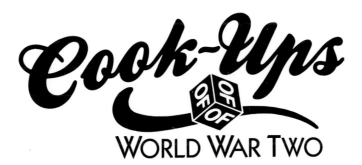

WORLD WAR TWO

BRYAN CHALKER

with photographs by
FELICITY HAZE

REDCLIFFE

Bristol

First published in 1987
by Redcliffe Press Ltd.,
49 Park St., Bristol

Text © Bryan Chalker
Photographs © Felicity Haze

ISBN 0 948265 66 3 case bound
ISBN 0 948265 36 1 paper bound

Typeset by Christie Typeset (UK) Ltd., Bristol
Printed by Penwell Ltd, Callington, Cornwall

CONTENTS

INTRODUCTION

The basic idea behind this book was born out of a series of radio programmes I wrote and presented a few years ago entitled 'The Roaring '40's'.

These programmes featured the popular music of World War Two, interwoven with the personal memories of people who lived during that era. The shows were extremely well received and I subsequently wrote a number of articles and stories on the subject for newspapers and magazines.

Over the course of the next few months I found myself becoming fascinated with the social history of the period and spent virtually a whole year researching and writing a book based upon my own recollections of the 1940's.

As I sifted through the reams of notes and photographs I had assembled for the final draft of the book, I discovered to my surprise that I had almost enough material to form the basis of a second book — on wartime cookery.

I completed the first book, A Child of Yesterday, in 1985, put it to one side for future reference and embarked upon my next project.

It quickly became clear to me that the subject of wartime cookery — particularly in those areas relating to the Kitchen Front — was sadly neglected in terms of definitive reference sources. In short, there were none, and my own notes fell far short of presenting a complete picture of that area of wartime activity.

I wrote to newspapers seeking assistance from readers old enough to remember the Second World War and contacted food manufacturers for the vital bits of information I needed to write a book. The response was tremendous and I received a wealth of data and long-forgotten recipes.

I am therefore especially indebted to Bovril Ltd., J. & J. Colman, Rowntree MacIntosh Sun-Pat Ltd. and General Foods Ltd., and to individuals like Jack Parkhouse, Dr. M.I.H. Clark, J.P., Lucy Meakins and Mrs. N. Storey, without whose assistance this book would not have been possible. I am also grateful to the *Bristol Evening Post*, *Western Daily Press* and the *Bath Evening Chronicle*, for publishing my requirements.

Another stumbling block presented itself when I decided to illustrate *Cook-Ups Of World War Two* with photographs of authentic wartime food tins and kitchen artifacts. They hardly fell into the category of 'antiques' and were consequently extremely difficult to find. I scoured flea markets, jumble sales, auctions, junk shops and car-boot sales in my quest for bygone products such as National Flour, powdered milk, dried eggs, Beefex, Marmite and Verox cubes, Rowntrees Cocoa, CWS Almond Custard Powder and oatmeal stout. One by one I managed to track them down until I became literally knee-deep in kitchen and larder memorabilia from the late 1930's and 40's. Enough, in fact, to kit out my own Mobile Canteen should the need ever arise!

Once the word was out that I was 'in

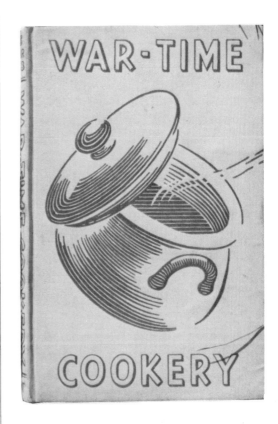

the market' for such objects, I became inundated with everything from ration books, SFP arm-bands and Identification Cards, to ARP helmets, gas masks — and a 45-year old bar of American cooking chocolate.

I should perhaps add that one of the primary motivations behind this book is the fact that virtually every recipe featured is as relevant today as it was forty to forty-five years ago. For many people this is still an age of austerity.

BRYAN CHALKER
Bath, 1987

5

THE KITCHEN FRONT

At the outset of hostilities in 1939, the food situation in Britain was critical. After nearly two years of waiting, Britain entered the Second World War largely unprepared for the massive problems of feeding her population of some forty-five million people.

Food rationing was a drastic but necessary wartime measure. But things weren't quite as bad as they first appeared. Certainly there were severe food restrictions and a wide range of food products vanished from the shelves of a country once described by Napoleon as 'a nation of shopkeepers'. Even G.K. Chesterton gently mocked the shopkeeping fraternity in Britain when he wrote *The Song Against Grocers*:

> God made the wicked grocer
> For a mystery and a sign,
> That men might shun the awful shops
> And go to inns to dine.

Indeed, Britain boasted some 700,000 shopkeepers by the end of the 1930's, but within a few years their numbers had been savagely reduced by Hitler's bombs.

The Ministry of Food, headed by the amiable Lord Woolton, saw to it that what food was available was equally and fairly apportioned. The nation as a whole actually benefitted from rationing. Suddenly Britain, deprived of meat and poultry (hens were needed for egg-laying and were far too valuable to kill), discovered the wholesome and beneficial virtues of vegetables. The potato, carrot and cabbage were immediately dubbed 'Home Guards of Health' by the Ministry of Food.

The allotment boom began in earnest as gardeners throughout the land grew every kind of edible crop imaginable. Parks, playing fields, flower gardens, race-courses, railway embankments and backyards were hastily cultivated in the drive to provide more food. Even the King's Great Park at Windsor became the biggest cornfield in Britain.

Although an allotment was defined as 'a parcel of land not more than two acres in extent, wholly or mainly cultivated by the occupier for the production of vegetable or fruit crops for his own or his family's consumption', allotments provided by local authorities during the war measured approximately thirty feet by ninety feet. Some were rented out for the equivalent of 15p a year, while others were as much as 50p a year. If that sounds trifling by today's standards, local authorities felt it necessary to point out to allotment holders that 'the charge is small compared with the profit gained'.

During the First World War more than two million allotments were under cultivation. By 1941 a total of five million allotments and gardens were being used to produce food.

'It is of no use to fine a farmer for leaving land under grass and ignoring great parklands, race-courses, sports grounds and private estates', said the Ministry of Agriculture in 1940. 'If the owners of such lands do not put them under cultivation, the Government should take them and do it for the owners, using the heavy fines that must be imposed as well as imprisonment in such cases to buy seed and implements'.

'Dig For Victory' and 'Grow More Food', urged an anxious but genuinely helpful Government. These slogans were aimed as much at 'the little man with the spade' as they were 'the big man with the plough'.

'Every endeavour must be made to grow the greatest volume of food of which this fertile island is capable', said Winston Churchill.

Within six months Britain's allotments had increased by a quarter of a million.

'Step On It!' became another official slogan, followed by these words of encouragement:

Dig Now — Don't Delay. Get your garden ready to grow your own vegetables — especially the kinds you can store. Apply to your local Council for an allotment and dig with all your might. Vegetables will be scarcer. Victory may well be won by the country with the most food. It is up to every man and woman to step on it now and make every garden a VICTORY GARDEN!

An ounce of food saved now is worth a pound at harvest time

The Ministry of Agriculture quickly issued a book called *Preserves from the Garden*. T.W. Sanders' *Kitchen Garden and Allotment*, which first appeared during the Great War, made a welcome re-appearance. The Wine and Food Society of London published *Vegetables*, edited by Andre L. Simon, as part of its *Concise Encyclopaedia of Gastronomy* series. Several volumes on preserving food were published by *Good Housekeeping* magazine. Penguin Books published *Food Growing, Storing and Cooking*, by F.W.P. Carter, a popular London journalist, and *Food — The Deciding Factor* by Frank Wokes.

Richard Sudell's earlier *Practical Gardening and Food Production*, published by Odhams Press, simplified the whole process of preparing the garden or allotment for wartime food production. The book even took into account the siting of the obligatory Anderson shelter — 'in an inconspicuous spot near the greenhouse', suggested the author.

Another popular gardening and allotment aid was C.H. Middleton's excellent *In Your Garden — Gardening at a*

Glance dial-chart, which was designed to pin to the wall for easy reference. The little device, made of strong cardboard and attractively printed in full colour, proved an invaluable aid to the amateur gardener.

The ever popular Mrs. Beeton's range of cookery books included one on the

subject of *Jam Making*, published in 1924. Featured in the book were hundreds of recipes for jams, preserves, marmalades, fruit jellies, crystallized fruit, pastes and curds, pickles and home-made wines.

As early as September 1939 the Ministry of Agriculture had taken swift measures to increase home food produc-tion by bringing additional farmland under the plough. By 1940 the Government aimed to increase such land in England and Wales by one and a half million acres.

Existing farmland was also improved, with counties like Nottinghamshire clearing 5,000 miles of farm ditches as part of the agricultural war effort to grow more food.

On the other hand, a total of 800,000 acres of good farmland were lost to the construction of wartime airfields.

It was estimated that a plot seven yards square could produce 160 pounds of food a year. If each family in Britain during the war had cultivated an addi-tional plot that size, an extra 850,000 tons of food could have been produced — about one hundred and seventy shiploads!

At that time Britain's normal annual consumption of food was approximately 26 million tons — the food required to feed a nation of some 45 million people.

About 15 per cent of food was wasted in the normal process of preparing and cooking and, while much of this was unavoidable, only one quarter of such waste needed to be eliminated by thoughtful planning and care — by using the clock and strict forms of measure — to save almost one million tons of food annually. Enough to feed the entire country for two weeks.

The war showed that, with an enor-mous combined effort, Britain could almost become a totally self-sufficient nation.

FIGHTING FIT

On September 6th, 1942, a Ministry of Food proclamation appeared in the nation's Sunday newspapers:

Fighting Fit — that's how we all want to feel now. The Ministry of Food has planned supplies to make this possible. It's food without frills, but that's right in wartime. Plan your family's meals to this fighting standard. Serve potatoes often — they're great energy givers and they save bread. Make the most of your cheese ration, it's a splendid body-builder, especially for children. Eat plenty of home-grown vegetables; they'll help to keep you fighting fit through the winter months. Food is your munition of war.

It was to be an era of gastronomic deprivation but, with innovation, imagination and a little applied intelligence, it taught the British how to cook and revived many old culinary skills.

The housewife of that era did not enjoy the benefits of the refrigerator to preserve food and milk, even though the earliest use dated back to 1895. At the outbreak of the war there were only just over 3,000 domestic refrigerators in Britain and full production did not start until after the war. Among the successful early refrigerators was the Guardian, of 1915, which had a self-contained freezing unit, a cabinet made of solid oak and used seaweed for insulation.

Frozen food itself had been introduced to Britain in 1937 by S.W. Smedley but was confined to hotels, restaurants and the few people fortunate enough to own a domestic refrigerator.

The task of preparing food for the family during wartime was made even more difficult by the recalling for scrap of every available piece of aluminium and iron, such as kettles, cutlery, saucepans, frying pans and teapots.

Breakfast cereals as we know them today had not really captured the nation's imagination. The breakfast cereal had originated in America during the mid-19th century and didn't find its way to Britain until 1914. At first breakfast cereals, which at that time included Grape Nuts, were not widely accepted in this country and the only British company to emerge between the two world wars was Weetabix. During World War Two it was possible to obtain Weetabix, Shredded Wheat, Corn Flakes, Force

Flakes and certain other cereals but this form of packaged food had not yet replaced the traditional British fried breakfast.

With the introduction of food rationing the potato came into its own, followed by the once humble cabbage. Carrots and onions were promoted to almost regal status for their apparently elixir-like qualities. Beetroot tops, elder flowers, dandelion leaves, stinging nettles, young ferns and marigolds began to find their way on to the nation's meal tables.

A wild spree of culinary discoveries followed as Britain embarked on a new eating age.

Britain's housewives and mothers, prompted by the challenge of making acceptable a severely reduced range of culinary raw materials, rallied to the cause with gusto and created a staggering array of recipes to combat rationing.

The national press and the Government referred to this cooking fervour as the Kitchen Front, or the Kitchen Army. In her popular *Wartime Cookery*, published in 1941, Hilda Neild wrote:

> The women's Kitchen Army is one of the most important sections of the women's fighting forces, though the members of it have no official status, wear no distinctive uniform,

armlets or Service badges . . .
Good feeding, ever a primary rule
for making a nation fit, is more than
ever necessary when there is a war
on; not only an army, but the whole
nation, marches to victory on its
stomach. The woman in the home
kitchen is doing equally useful work
as any woman in khaki or blue . . .

The Government's popular and long-
running series of *Our Food Today*
leaflets and *Food Facts* became a way
of life for housewives eager to brighten
dull wartime fare. The latter series,
which appeared in most daily
newspapers and women's magazines of
the period, included advice on how to
obtain the best results from National
Dried Milk, dried whole eggs and
vegetables, and featured a host of simple recipes for puddings, pickles,
desserts, main courses and chutneys.

The Association of Teachers of
Domestic Subjects published *Cookery in
Wartime* in 1940, later re-naming it
Hard Time Cookery. This booklet contained chapters on the principles of diet,
practical hints for catering, economy in
the use of fuel, and suggestions for dealing with a shortage of certain foods.

Other publications from the same
source included *The A.T.D.S. Cookery
Book*, *Meat Dishes at Small Cost* and
School Dinners. The first title featured
several chapters on the various methods
of cooking, such as boiling, steaming,
stewing, roasting, baking, braising and
frying, the feeding of infants and
children, camp cookery and the preparation of cheese, eggs, puddings, pastry,
salads, fish, meat, soups and stocks.
Among the suggested recipes were Cabbage Soup, Fish Pudding, Haddock,
Stuffed and Baked, Boiled Sheep's Head,
Jugged Rabbit and Durham Cutlets. Also
included were valuable hints on the daily
care of the cooking range and gas and
electric cookers. The chapter devoted to
ranges and cookers opened:

The modern type of coal range is
much easier to work with than the
old-fashioned stove, which was
cumbersome, extravagant and
troublesome to clean. Heat storage
cookers are becoming popular, and
though expensive to buy, are
labour-saving and economical in the
use of fuel.

Where gas and/or electricity are available, gas and/or electric stoves have largely taken the place of coal ranges, while in country districts, if neither is available, oil stoves are commonly used.

The BBC's Radio Doctor, later Lord Hill, broadcasting after the eight o'clock news each morning, was among a veritable army of experts dispensing advice and recommending innovative cuts of meat. The Radio Doctor often promoted the merits of a certain Lancashire delicacy – tripe – once described by a national newspaper columnist as 'Liver struck by lightning'.

S.P.B.Mais, another regular BBC broadcaster, gave advice on how best to cope with limited food supplies.

One of the most prolific writers of wartime cookery books was Ambrose Heath, whose publisher, Hutchinson & Co., listed a total of seventeen on the inside front cover of his *The Good Cook in Wartime*.

The Good Cook in Wartime, which sold for one shilling and contained forty pages, placed its emphasis on *good* cooking and 'better meals with less fuel'.

Ambrose Heath did not pull any punches when referring to Britain's characteristic method of over-cooking everything:

One of the things that most easily and most often ruins good food is indiscriminate use of heat. A stew boiled is a stew spoiled, they say; but many other foods are spoiled too by thoughtless carelessness; potatoes are galloped to pieces, fish is boiled to shreds, greens are cooked until they are waterlogged. It has taken a world war to teach us something about combining good food with healthy meals.

The book highlighted the versatility of the potato, and the adaptability of fish and meat. Included were such recipes as Potato and Jerusalem Artichoke Soup, Curried Fish Salad, Fluffy Cabbage and Sweet Slices.

Ambrose Heath also advocated the use of the haybox method of cooking food, but more about that later.

Josephine Terry's *Food without Fuss* featured creations like Carrot Bread, Herring and Potato Mustard, Pink Potato Soup and Hedgehogs, which were simple biscuits made with flour, potato, cinnamon, baking powder, salt and, 'if one could possibly afford it', a little milk and a few grains of sugar.

A Ministry of Food leaflet, *Wise Housekeeping in War-Time*, suggested sensible ways of saving fats, sugar, bread and fuel and advised housewives to 'listen to the wireless for announcements about the supplies of various foodstuffs', and to 'watch the shops and take advantage of seasonal foods'. It also urged the housewife to look in the larder before setting out for the shops; in that way an economical purchasing pattern could be established.

A popular BBC programme was called 'The Kitchen Front', hosted by such personalities as Mabel Constanduros and Freddie Grisewood.

Wartime cookery publications and

radio broadcasts catered for the Kitchen Front's every requirement. There were practical guides for the use of canned foods, supper dishes, egg and milk recipes (one booklet contained 151 recipes using milk and included Semolina Sunflowers, Milk Jelly, Carrot Pie and Scrambled Onions), economical meat dishes and the use of cheese.

There was even a cheaply produced, 16-page, *Daily Mirror* booklet called, *Take a Look . . . And be a Cook — Kitchen Sense for Men*, which stated in no uncertain terms that the sight of a man paddling helplessly and ineffectually round the kitchen was not funny. The book also considered it quite deplorable that men could act so dumb. 'Neither are we moved to pity by the mess he gets himself, the food and the kitchen into', the book continued acidly.

Between the barbed humour and cartoon drawings of hen-pecked men, were countless commonsense suggestions for making tea and coffee properly, preparing greens, timing various dishes, and essential kitchen cleanliness.

The writer — obviously a woman — did nothing to endear herself to her potential readers, however, and from beginning to end the book is an aggressive put-down of 'domesticated' man.

'We know you're going to see right off that not being able to cook even an egg is fine and dandy when you've got someone else to look after you. But when you haven't, and you're hungry — not so funny, is it?', reads one passage.

'You have probably always thought that making tea was merely a matter of slapping a few leaves into the tea-pot and then chucking in some water', it continues mercilessly. 'In your ignorance, you've probably thought that there was no such thing as method in cooking. You just slap a few things together, clang a

lot of pans about, and there you are — you thought', and so on.

Fortunately most wartime cookery books refrained from such rabid sexism, although several were written in a fairly light, humorous vein, or contained cooking methods and household hints that appear amusing today.

The British Medical Association issued a handbook entitled *The Doctors Tell You What to Eat in War-Time.*

The doctors of Great Britain want to take their full share in helping the country in these grave times. They are caring for the sick and wounded, and they also want to assist the healthy to maintain their strength and well-being. The keystone of good health is good food.

The handbook itself dispelled a number of popular myths of the time, including the belief that drinking milk was effeminate. It also promoted the nutritional value of the now revered potato.

'The appearance of the potato has been against it', stated the B.M.A., 'and it has not received the recognition due to it as a most excellent food. If we in this country were limited to two foods, probably

the best choice would be potatoes and milk (some of it made into butter and cheese).'

Among the sound advice the book offered was that people could live 'quite beneficially on a diet of brown bread, cheese and milk, with fresh fruit or salad daily.'

The Doctors' Cookery Book was another British Medical Association publication. It strove to promote 'national fitness by improving nutrition in the home' and was therefore ideally suited to wartime conditions. The book suggested that 'if you cannot afford to cook every day, by careful selection you will find it possible to do two days' cooking at a time'. The recipes included Stewed Tripe and Onions, Steamed Plum Duff, Fried Herrings and Sea Pie.

Another invaluable publication was *The National Food Fund Handbook for Housewives*, or *How to Save Money in War Time*.

First published at the end of the First World War, this compact little handbook was still fairly relevant a generation later. The objects of the book were to 'prevent waste of the National Food Resources' and to aid in 'the collection and distribution of food through the agency of approved societies dealing

with distress caused by the War'.

In its prefatory note, the book made it quite clear that its message was aimed at the middle classes:

> The cooks and mistresses of the richer households are, it will be seen, omitted, equally with the very poor town-dwelling housewives . . .

It was stressed by the Government in 1939, and throughout the war years, that the peeling of potatoes was a peacetime luxury and destroyed natural roughage, and that food value was lost through over-cooking.

The 1939 edition of M. Bircher Benner and Max E. Bircher's book, *Fruit Dishes and Raw Vegetables*, was a useful alternative to those desiring food which had not been 'denatured by heat or the extraction of certain properties in cooking'. The authors referred to their

preparation of fruit and vegetables as 'sunlight food'.

The Government, through its Ministry of Food, however, was keen to promote the various *proper* methods of *cooking* vegetables, as well as examining the nutritional properties of the raw variety.

'Not only are they valuable food, but properly cooked or attractively served raw, vegetables are delicious, full of variety and capable of being used in a number of different ways', said the Ministry.

'Serve a good big helping of any green vegetables every day. Greens should be cooked quickly; served at once; keeping hot or warming up lessens their value', they warned. 'Serve also a good portion of root vegetables. Be sure that carrots are served several times a week. When cooking potatoes, boil or steam them in their skins for utmost health value'.

Those who have the will to win,
Cook potatoes in their skin:
Knowing that the sight of peelings,
Deeply hurts Lord Woolton's
feelings.

A contemporary wag, familiar with the British practice of abusing and misusing garden produce, suggested that English cooking demanded the formation of a Society for the Prevention of Cruelty to Vegetables.

'We can produce enough vegetables in our country to feed the whole nation,' the Ministry of Food had claimed at the onset of the war. 'The main thing to remember in cooking vegetables is to bring them to the table as near their normal selves, and with as much of their natural goodness as possible. Cook them in a steamer if you can; they will retain their flavour'.

'Fighting Fit' became the battle cry of the nation from 1939.

The National Union of Teachers prepared a publication called *School Canteen Handbook*, which featured this 'healthy' meal for an elementary school child: 'Potato Milk Soup, Health Sandwich, salad, nuts and raisins and water'. The *Health Sandwich*, it should be noted, was made from wholemeal bread and margarine, with a filling of yeast, cress and chopped cheese, egg or liver. With snacks like that on the menu, it was small wonder that so many children

disliked school meals.

Professor Drummond, Scientific Adviser to the Ministry of Food, said:

What we've all got to realise is that little differences of diet may make all the difference in winning the war. To be fighting fit we've all got to drink a little more milk, eat a little more cheese, and much more green food and fruit — it's easy, it's cheap, and it's pleasant. We're going to come out of this war better fed than we were when we went in, richer in the commonsense way of eating.

He was right. The frugal but carefully thought out wartime diet really did improve the nation's health. Deaths from tuberculosis and the infant mortality rate both dropped considerably.

The health of the nation was also improved by the increase of milk supplied through the National Milk Scheme to expectant mothers and young children, and the distribution of orange juice and cod liver oil for children. These combined to produce a strong new generation of Britons.

Lord Woolton himself exercised diplomacy, tact and wit in dealing with the public and his Ministry quickly earned the grudging respect of the nation. The highly efficient Lord created his own economical dish — Lord Woolton Pie — made from parsnips, pastry and the ubiquitous potato. It resembled a meatless Cornish pasty and the contents could be varied as different vegetables came into season.

By 1942 Lord Woolton was able to say that 'Ever since I have been Minister of Food I have taken the pessimistic view of the food situation. If I hadn't you wouldn't be so well off now. The war may be long, and wise people prepare for the worst. Put by what you can even from the comparatively meagre rations you are getting. We have plenty of food in this country. We have husbanded it with great care. But I do beg of you to

be careful with it, because without food we should lose the war'.

Several months earlier Lord Woolton had written:

It is good to think that posterity will learn from those who had to cater in Britain's front line. After all, housewives are war-workers same as anybody else, aren't they?

The Ration Book allocation of food was meagre and amounted to a quarter of a pound of tea, two ounces of butter, two ounces of cheese, five ounces of margarine, eight ounces of sugar, two ounces of lard, two and a half pints of milk, four ounces of bacon and three ounces of sweets! During the early years of the war a family was allowed one packet of dried eggs a month per Ration Book, but by February 1944 this had been increased to two packets.

Within a few months of the outbreak of war, hundreds of cookery books and pamphlet were issued by the Ministry of Food via its Food Advice Division, daily newspapers, women's magazines and

food manufacturers. Publications produced by the *Daily Star*, the *Daily Mirror*, *Vogue* magazine, Be-Ro Flour, Stork Margarine, *Good Housekeeping* magazine, Marmite, Oxo, Borwick's Baking Powder, His Majesty's Stationery Office, Colman's Mustard, Symington's, *Home Notes* magazine and McDougall's Flour, were among the

most popular. But perhaps the most widely read of all cookery books were the numerous volumes by the legendary Mrs. Beeton.

Almost every daily newspaper and women's magazine featured cookery columns, shopping guides and gardening hints. Each column was aimed directly at the Kitchen Front in one way or another.

Two cartoon strips, *Adam the Gardener* and *Mr Digwell* − the latter is still featured in the Daily Mirror to this day − were also widely read.

In 1941, the Ministry of Information published a booklet written by Guy Reed entitled, *The Little Less . . . And How Much It Is*, which contained hundreds of fascinating facts and figures relating to food rationing and its effect on the Kitchen Front and the war effort in general. For example, a rationing of 8 oz sugar a week meant that the saving in sugar imports amounted to 570,000 tons a year; a total of one hundred and fourteen ships would have been required to transport that much sugar to Britain. Even with rationing, over one million tons of sugar were consumed annually in British homes during World War Two!

By rationing meat, bacon and tea, the nation made a saving in shipping space of 500,000 tons a year − equivalent to

the cargoes of one hundred ships!

It wasn't long before a National Food Campaign was organised by the Government, and munitions works, Gas and Electricity companies and Educational Authorities, among others, staged demonstrations of economy cooking with what were described at the time as 'the dullest, cheapest ingredients', using such patriotic titles as *Kitchen Garden Backs Kitchen Front*.

The National Food Campaign also offered refresher courses for housewives on such subjects as 'How to plan balanced meals for good health', 'Which foods to use to save the country's shipping' and 'What to pack for the workers' lunch'.

All the time Lord Woolton and his Ministry of Food urged the nation to reduce its waistline to increase its

lifeline.

To make identification easier food was graded in different coloured containers at official cookery demonstrations – grey for *Protective* foods such as greens and wheatmeal bread; red for *Fuel-forming* potatoes and sugar; and bright blue for *Body-building* produce and food like cheese, fish and eggs. That measure alone was an indication of how the former culinary skills of the British had been gradually eroded over the years.

Housewives were also encouraged to buy frozen fish as often as possible. By 1940 the frozen fish industry in Britain was booming, because of the difficulties of fishing in home waters and the demand created by meat rationing. Frozen fish from abroad included salmon, cod, halibut, plaice, lemon sole and crawfish. Frozen fish was considerably cheaper than fresh, for obvious reasons.

Among the popular fresh fish was the herring, because of its great versatility and pleasing flavour. The herring has been called 'Nature's own health food', because of its high protein value. As a wartime food the herring, when available, was invaluable. It could be grilled, fried, baked, stewed, braised, pickled or boiled – and its roe, both soft and hard, was highly nutritious. One pound of herrings contains 755 calories, against 685 for the same amount of meat. It is no surprise, therefore, that so many wartime recipes featured the herring.

'When you eat herring you are getting at a very low price all the merits of cod liver oil, and with a delicious instead of a disagreeable flavour', said a wartime doctor.

The herring appeared in two other guises, of course — the traditional kipper and bloater. Herring recipes abound in wartime cookery books. Among the most popular were Herring Pie, Herrings au Gratin, Scalloped Herring, Soft Roe Potato Cakes and Herrings in Cream Sauce.

Greater use was made, too, of tinned fish and instead of carelessly scooping out the contents of a tin of sardines or pilchards and leaving the oil or sauce for the family cat or dog, every little drop was put to nutritional use during the war years. The oil from sardines or pilchards could be mixed with mashed potato and fried to form mock fish-cakes. Some housewifes resorted to using cod liver oil blended with mashed potato for the same purpose!

THE BRITISH RESTAURANT

Despite food rationing people were still able to eat out for, curiously enough, restaurant meals were unrationed. This was due, no doubt, to the reluctance of Neville Chamberlain's Government to encroach on the traditional pleasures of the middle and upper classes.

For the first year of two of the war British Railways even managed to maintain a catering standard of sorts by offering a traditional three-course breakfast of kippers or fried fish, followed by bacon and eggs, or a grill, with toast and marmalade.

In London's West End it was possible to dine at the Winston Hotel's Auberge de France Restaurant in Piccadilly for the modest sum of 5s. 6d. Dinner at the Café Anglais was a few shillings dearer at 8s. 6d. and Harry Roy and his Band were thrown in for good measure. The Dorchester Hotel was rather more up-market, with dinner or supper for 12s. 6d., but with the added attraction of the popular Maurice Win-

nick & The Dorchester Hotel Band for dancing between the hours of 8.30 pm and 1.00 am — subject to air raids. In Leicester Square the New Queen's Brasserie offered lunch at a very modest 3s. 6d.

On June 23rd, 1940, however, one newspaper columnist condemned the lack of restrictions on restaurant food:

> We cannot afford the tickling of palates. All the hotels and restaurants should now be on restricted menus. This will prevent the food wastage involved in long menus and the money the gourmets

save can be lent to the Government. More important, the restriction will ensure a more equitable share-out of what food there is.

Bowing to public and media pressure by 1942, the Government was obliged to set about providing communal eating places for the less privileged members of society.

It was Winston Churchill who instigated the famous British Restaurants which, by the end of 1943, were providing their customers with an amazing 600,000 meals a day!

These establishments were located in drill halls, scouts' huts, assembly rooms, abandoned warehouses, schools and even the hallowed galleries of London's stately Victoria & Albert Museum. In Bath the city's elegant and historic Pump Rooms were turned over to the serving of communal meals. The food was prepared in Bristol, packed in vacuum containers and hayboxes and transported by van to Bath for distribution.

A two-course meal containing a pennyworth of meat 'off the ration', suet

pudding and a generous helping of vegetables, could be had for the equivalent of 2½p. A pint mug of hot tea was a penny extra!

In other areas devastated by intense bombing and unable to provide suitable premises for British Restaurants, emergency field kitchens and mobile canteens were set up and manned by members of the Women's Voluntary Services, the Y.M.C.A., the Salvation Army, the Red Cross and other groups. Cargoes of food arrived in colourful vans supplied by the Queen's Messenger Convoys and were distributed by groups of willing volunteers.

America gave Britain one hundred mobile canteens for use in the London area but these vehicles were eventually pooled and their work centrally co-ordinated.

The W.V.S. took their mobile canteens out under the bombs with refreshments for civil defenders and anyone else needing it. 'We had a choice of being frozen, burned, blown up, or drowned in tea', reported one fireman at the time.

The dangers were many and mobile canteens frequently returned to base with their radiators, windscreens and driver's cabs peppered with holes made by machine-gun bullets or bomb fragments — or were lost altogether.

'No one is refused', became the motto of the field kitchens and mobile canteens. Meals and cups of tea and cocoa were served to anyone who came along. Special vans dispensed tea day and night, irrespective of whether bombs were falling or not.

There were said to be two universal solaces for those suffering from blitz strain, minor injuries, or mild shellshock — tea and *telling* about it.

At the Rest Centre, the mobile canteen on the blitzed street corner, or the wrecked kitchen at home, the good old

cup of tea was the British currency of sympathy and comfort.

In London's heavily bombed dockland areas Church of England clergy, collaborating with the London County Council, set up a canteen in a bomb damaged school and managed to provide A.F.S. men, A.R.P. workers and homeless families with up to 1,000 meals a day.

After the May 1941 raids on Hull, when many public and private warehouses containing food were destroyed, a large emergency food store was put out of action, and two large bakeries were razed to the ground, emergency services managed to prepare and serve an incredible total of 460,000 meals in eighteen days.

A similar catering miracle occurred in Sheffield in 1941, when the staff of the Institution at Fir Vale turned out no fewer than 6,000 meals in one twenty-four hour period and continued to serve the city's homeless for several days to come.

In naval towns and ports, groups of sailors went out as Friendly Aid Parties, assisting the public in every possible way. They comforted the injured and homeless, repaired broken windows, swept up fallen plaster, made tea and dispensed food.

All large air raid shelters had their own canteens but in areas of almost total devastation improvised meals were prepared and served from hastily dug cooking trenches.

In London, Bristol, Bath, Portsmouth, Coventry, Birmingham, Sheffield, Manchester, Swansea, Cardiff, Middlesborough, Canterbury, Hull, Dover, Plymouth, Belfast, Clydeside, Southampton and other towns and cities throughout the British Isles, the picture was the same.

'It is cheaper – and better – to eat together', said Mr. Robert Boothby, Parliamentary Secretary to the Ministry of Food. 'Lord Woolton', he added, 'had expressed interest in the development of communal feeding not only as a wartime measure, but also as a long-term policy – a permanent and beneficial feature of national life in Britain.'

By May 1940, the Government had approved the publication of the Women's Voluntary Services' book, *Communal Feeding In War Time*, which contained valuable advice on 'canteen diets for children and adults who eat in communal canteens', and urged the liberal use of menus which provided the necessary vitamins to keep a nation fit during wartime.

In just seventy pages the book describes in detail every facet of communal feeding, from the basic organization of finance, rationing and staff, to the setting up of the canteen, the catering and elementary principles of nutrition.

Where mobile canteens were being started, they were supposed to be able to cater for up to 400 people on light

BLACK-OUT ZERO HOUR TO-NIGHT UNTIL 4.59 A.M.

MOON 7.49 RISES P.M. MOON 4.17 SETS A.M.

rations without restocking. A car of not less than 16 h.p. — and fitted with a proper tow-bar — was needed to draw each caravan.

The book also suggested that horse boxes were quite suitable for adapting as food and drink transporters and advocated the use of vacuum containers and the haybox, an old method of heating food now fallen into general disuse. The instructions for the making of a haybox were:

To construct a haybox, line a good-sized sugar case with several layers of strong paper, pasted in, and cover the outside with American cloth. It is best to have an overlapping lid hinged and lined in the same way. Make a hay cushion to lay over the top of the containers and fit a hasp to keep the lid tightly down. Use earthenware pots as containers if possible. Bring all food to the boil before placing in the box and then pack tightly round with hay; place hay cushion on top and fasten the lid. There should always be a four-inch thickness of hay between the vessels and the sides of the box. For the purpose of keeping liquids hot (but not cooking) containers must be full, but the hay box should not be tightly packed with hay.

The Ministry of Food issued more detailed instructions:

Choose a strong packing case with a lid, or a tin box with a hasp lock. Even an old trunk will serve the purpose. Line it well with clean

newspaper; cover the lining with clean felt or old blanket if possible. If not, with more newspaper. Follow the same procedure with the lid, padding it well. Then fill the box with clean hay. If you have a lawn you can make your own hay from the cuttings.

Make a hay cushion four inches deep, to fit the inner section beneath the lid.

Arrange the hay in tight packing to reach within four inches of the top. Part the hay to make a nest for each pan. Short-handled pans with tight fitting lids are best. Space the nests four inches apart. The number of nests that you can manage depends, of course, on the size of the box. Fill the pans with boiling water; put on their lids and place them in the nests. Cover with the cushion and leave for some hours. After this, the nests will keep their shape for the pans.

The haybox was used in the following manner:

Bring the food to the boil in a saucepan on the stove. Secure the lid tightly, then wrap the pan quickly and compactly in newspaper before you place it in the nest. Cover it with the cushion and fasten down the lid. Do not open the box again until the cooking is completed. After the dish is removed from the haybox, reheat for a few minutes. This is especially necessary after a long period of cooking, as for porridge or stew.

These were the recommended cooking times issued during World War Two:

	On the stove	In the haybox
Vegetable soups (dried peas, etc.)	45 minutes	4 hours
Potato or root vegetable soup	15 minutes	1¼ hours
Plain meat stew	30 minutes	3½ hours
Meat pudding	45 minutes (boiling)	3 hours
Oatmeal porridge	5 minutes	6 hours (or overnight)
Stewed rice	2-3 minutes	2½ hours
Stewed dried fruit	2-3 minutes	3½ hours
Stewed fresh fruit (apples, etc.)	2-3 minutes	1½ hours
Suet pudding	30 minutes (boiling)	2½ hours

The haybox was particularly suitable for use in mobile canteens and emergency kitchens.

With so many hungry mouths to feed from such limited resources, it wasn't surprising that tempers sometimes frayed

at the edges. A Birmingham chef in charge of a large canteen claimed that Birmingham people did not understand or appreciate food.

'All they want is fish and chips, bread and butter and brown gravy over everything', he told a news reporter bitterly. 'They won't eat salads, don't like savouries and didn't like the white sauce I made with the boiled beef and carrots', he concluded sadly.

By and large the efforts of the mobile canteen cooks and the countless thousands of women attached to the Kitchen Army produced results that were more than appreciated by their customers and families.

POTATOES
feed without fattening and give
you *ENERGY*

POTATOES WITH EVERYTHING

Many families, although suffering from extensive bomb damage to their homes, disliked communal feeding and preferred to stay put and improvise over open fires, hastily repaired domestic gas appliances, or primitive Tommy's cookers and primus stoves.

A Clydebank man, rather than waste household gas, filled a saucepan with milk, rushed into the street where an incendiary bomb lay blazing and boiled the milk over the flames!

Humour was in evidence throughout the war and it seemed that nothing could possibly quell the British resolve for getting on with the job, come what may. Following a second air raid on the street where she lived, an elderly London woman is reported to have called to a neighbour from her splintered front door, 'Well, there's one thing about these raids — they do make yer forget about the bleedin' war'.

Another Londoner, her home almost completely destroyed by enemy action, escaped unscathed and relentlessly scrubbed and polished her doorstep each morning — the only part of the house

to remain intact — and left a daily note out for the milkman!

On April 12th, 1941, Winston Churchill said:

> I see the damage done by the enemy attacks; but I also see, side by side with the devastation and amid the ruins, quiet, confident, bright and smiling eyes, beaming with a consciousness of being associated with a cause far higher and wider than any human or personal issue. I see the spirit of an unconquerable people.

In the meantime the tireless and endlessly harassed members of Britain's glorious Kitchen Army — the nation's wartime housewives — quietly and confidently went about their business.

On the Kitchen Front, alternative recipes were soon in abundance. Many women employed great imagination in creating mouth-watering soups, puddings and other dishes from watercress, runner bean leaves, tansy, lovage, sorrel, elderberries, rose petals, borage and chestnuts. They discovered new ways of preparing and serving potatoes, cabbage, parsnips and other previously neglected root vegetables.

In September 1942, thirty leading chefs held a competition in London to invent new and appealing ways of cooking potatoes. The results were eventually passed on to the housewife through the medium of cookery columns and Ministry of Food advertisements in the national press and women's magazines.

'Potatoes keep you fighting fit' and 'Potatoes are part of the battle', were two old wartime campaign slogans aimed at promoting the potato to a higher status in the kitchen.

The potato became the Kitchen Army's most important weapon. After decades of abuse and misuse and an almost complete lack of appreciation from Britain's home cooks, the humble spud suddenly became the King among vegetables.

The *Concise Encyclopaedia of Gastronomy* had this to say about the potato:

> The flavour of the potato is not aggressive, and yet it holds its own against all comers, be it steam or boiling water, sizzling butter, olive oil or any kind of fat. This is why there are more and more varied manners of cooking potatoes than all other vegetables, as one can easily ascertain by consulting any cookery book. There is only one thing that cookery books do not tell us, and that is how to boil potatoes.

As a staple food the potato has a long and fascinating history. Originating in South America, it was discovered during the 16th century by Spanish explorers travelling through Peru. In their travels the Spaniards found that the principle food eaten by the people of Peru was vegetarian, mainly maize, ground-nuts, tomatoes, beans, manioc, sweet potatoes, avocados – and potatoes.

Centuries earlier the Peruvians had discovered a method of preserving potatoes by freezing and drying immediately following the harvest.

The potatoes were harvested, cleaned of soil, and laid out on the ground to expose them to the extremely cold Peruvian night air. The following day groups of natives would literally tread the moisture from the potatoes. This process was repeated for several days until the vegetables were completely dried by the natural action of the sun. The potatoes were then stored in a dry place until required. In this dried form the potatoes were known to the Peruvians as chuñu and formed an important part of their diet.

Such methods of food preservation by

natural means had been known since prehistoric times but it wasn't until the second half of the 19th century that artificial freezing methods were invented.

Freezing food on a commercial basis did not appear until the 1920's when an American, Clarence Birdseye, refined the process by which food is brought into immediate contact with cold metal plates. Birdseye's product, called Birdseye Frozen Foods, was introduced to Britain in 1938 but by that time several British companies, like Smethurst and Smedleys, were already marketing frozen food on a commercial basis.

Perhaps the most important and certainly the oldest form of food preservation in commercial use today is that of dehydration. Before 1945, however, the commercial production of dehydrated food was confined to a small selection of food, such as peas, beans and a variety of soups. Captain James Cook took a stock of such food with him on his epic voyage round the world in the 18th century.

The Spaniards obviously studied the Peruvian methods of drying and preserving potatoes in great depth, because the potato was quickly adopted by the Spanish Navy as basic ship's 'stores', and the vegetable was then introduced to

Spain, Italy and later to other European countries.

The potato reached England, however, by way of Virginia, with the assistance of Sir Francis Drake, or so the story goes.

In 1586, Drake was engaged in transporting a number of starving settlers from Virginia to England. On the way there Drake was obliged to anchor at the Colombian port of Cartegena to take on stores, which included potatoes. The English colonists whom Sir Francis Drake 'rescued' from Virginia took a quantity of these potatoes back across the Atlantic to England, where the vegetable was initially greeted with great enthusiasm.

For a time, at least, the potato was considered to be quite fashionable and was accredited with curing 'fluxes of the bowels' and 'increasing the seed and provoking lust'.

Later authorities claim that a Mr. Heriot was responsible for the introduction of the potato to England. The potato was certainly grown here at the end of the 16th century and Gerarde, in his *Herbal*, gives credence to the former story by referring to the vegetable as the 'Potato of Virginia', and claims that he grew it in the garden of his waterside home in London.

Following its initial acceptance in England, the potato then spent the best part of two hundred years in relative obscurity before its true food value was discovered. The potato was an extremely useful crop in Ireland, as it grew underground and was therefore not at risk at the hands of marauders during the

country's troubled history.

The traditional Irish method of boiling potatoes is in their jackets. The Irish usually cut a small piece from the potato at its thickest end before boiling; this allows the steam to escape and thus prevents cracking.

During the Second World War the Government went to great lengths to educate the housewife in the correct methods of cooking potatoes and deriving the full benefits from them. It was made quite clear that 'the most economical and nutritive way of boiling potatoes is to do them in their jackets'. Putting them into *boiling* water in their skins reduced waste and the loss of vitamins and mineral salts was reduced to a minimum.

Round the clock energy

The Government's intensive campaign to promote the wholesome virtues of *all* vegetables was founded on common sense and a high degree of solid medical evidence. With careful planning and thoughtful preparation it was quite possible for the nation during wartime to survive on a meatless diet without harmful results.

Several examples of longevity apparently attributable to meatless diets were used to support the Government's 'Eat More Vegetables' policy.

A certain George Broadbent, of Dobcross, had lived to the ripe old age of 98 on a diet of 'milk-meats and home-grown vegetables'.

In Elizabethan times Thomas Parr, known as 'Old Parr', reputedly attained the incredible age of 152 on a diet of 'sub-rancid cheese, and milk in every form, coarse and hard bread and small, generally sour whey'. In truth Parr probably lived to about 90. A Venetian nobleman, Luigi Cornara, who died in 1566 at the age of 98 was said to have survived for countless years on 'one egg, some milk and 14 oz. of wine a day'.

It was also claimed that George Bernard Shaw attributed his longevity — he was 92 — to living 'without tasting fish, flesh or fowl'.

Unfortunately, there is no medical evidence to support the claims. An old Yorkshire saying has it that 'no meal is complete without something on the plate that's drawn breath'.

In 1767, John Hanway wrote: 'The food of the poor is good bread, cheese, peas and turnips in winter, with a little pork or other meat when they can afford it.'

Over a hundred and seventy two years later John Hanway's advice was still basically sound.

Throughout the Government's Campaign vegetables were also given child-appeal with the help of colourful cartoon characters like Popeye (for spinach), Clara Carot, Dr. Carrot and Potato Pete, whose catchphrase was 'Step Lively With Me'. There was even an official *Potato Pete's Recipe Book*.

GROW FOOD FOR THE NATION
FEEDING STUFFS FOR YOUR FARMS
KEEP OUR SHIPS AND MONEY FREE
FOR BUYING VITAL ARMS

THE NATIONAL
LOAF

Wartime hoarding of food was illegal and the courts secured a number of convictions against members of the public and retailers who flouted the law. Gradually the Government, with the help of the national press and the severity of the fines, persuaded the public that such practices, along with black-marketeering, were not only illegal but socially unacceptable.

'Deliberate offences against the food orders are, fortunately, very rare', said a Ministry of Food spokesman in 1942. 'To buy on the black market today is not merely an offence, it is worse — it is bad form. If food distribution has succeeded, it is because of the willing co-operation of the trades and of the public. The law-abiding habit of the people of this country has been the department's greatest asset'.

It wasn't so much that the Government's campaign against black-marketeering in food had succeeded, but that the black-marketeers themselves became more wily and avoided prosecution.

That the Government succeeded in reducing the number of rationing offences involving the general public, however, could not be disputed. Newspapers of the time reveal widely varying fines relating to such offences.

In 1941, three Bromley women were each fined ten shillings for buying meat in excess of their ration allocation. The company supplying the meat — J. Sainsbury — was fined £4.

A Westmorland magistrate, on the other hand, was fined a total of £450 in 1943, for buying ham in excess of the controlled price and rationed food above the authorized quantity. Another man convicted of hoarding excessive quantities of food was fined an incredible £750, and such heavy penalties obviously acted as effective deterrents.

The Government put its message across in other, more subtle ways. To emphasize the social 'unacceptability' of defying the law, the Ministry of Food introduced the following 'statement' from a fictitious butcher into one of its wartime advertisements:

And then there's this trying to wangle a bit extra to the ration. It's asking me to get into trouble, but that's not the worst of it. It's downright selfish and it's downright unpatriotic. Giving a helping hand to Hitler, that's what I call it.

Losing face with friends and

neighbours in those days was a grave social misdemeanour, particularly if one's actions were in the slightest way unpatriotic.

Hoarding might have been illegal but 'putting a bit aside all the time', as Lord Woolton put it, was greatly encouraged.

'I have kept you short deliberately for some months, during which time I have been doing what the ordinary housewife does – putting a bit aside all the time', Lord Woolton told the press in May 1942. 'When we think of the raw materials and the food materials that came from places now in the hands of Japan, and of the dangers of the sea, it will be realized that our troubles are not likely to decrease', he warned.

'The line of Food Defence runs through all our homes. It is where we must always be on our guard. The watchword is careful housekeeping. It may seem so simple, this urgent duty, that we may tend to overlook its full meaning. A little saving here and there – how can that really help us to win the war? A little here and there, with our 45,000,000 people all contributing, becomes an immense amount. Take one example. Many people make tea by allowing one teaspoonful a head, and an additional teaspoon 'for the pot'. The teaspoon 'for the pot' is unnecessary. It is equal over the whole population to sixty shiploads a year. We must have those ships to bring munitions. Remember how much of our food comes from overseas – more than 20 million tons in a peacetime year. Let us picture the convoys, bringing the cargoes to our shores and let us be very careful', Lord Woolton concluded.

Thrifty housewives faced with great food reductions in the quantities of meat, eggs, sugar and canned foods available to them, simply learned to improvise and supplement without totally depleting their weekly rations.

Rhubarb juice was found to be a satisfactory and pleasing substitute for lemon juice. Parsnips, rich in natural sugar, could be cooked in a variety of ways; freshly grated turnip, if quickly used, would make do when the pepper supply ran out. Grated beetroot could be used to sweeten tea; potatoes could be turned into flour suitable for pastry, or mashed and used to thicken soups and stews.

Spinach, young dandelions, nasturtium leaves, cowslip leaves and chopped cabbage were found to be excellent additions to salads and lettuce leaves were useful for thickening soups and broths. The outer leaves of cabbages – usually discarded without a second thought – were useful additions to soups and stocks. And so it went on.

Ironically the Germans, who provided Britain with the blueprint for her own successful food rationing programme, also proved to be imaginative when it came to making the most of an unexpected opportunity. In 1943, Berliners actually ate zebra and elephant meat, when animals escaping from the city's zoo after an R.A.F. bombing raid, were shot by soldiers.

In 1939, one cheeky Welshman attempted to turn the impending food shortage to his advantage by claiming exemption from military service on the dubious grounds that he was 'doing work of national importance'. It transpired that he was working in a pickle factory. His appeal was deferred by a South Wales tribunal.

The 1940's quickly developed into an era of spam, Tang, National Dried Milk, National Flour, Glucose-D, dried eggs, meagre meat and sugar rations, air raid sirens, Anderson shelters, the National Loaf — and ration books.

The National Loaf became an institution and was described as 'the pride and joy of the Ministry of Food'. It was promoted as 'the best bread in Europe, and the only unrationed loaf in Europe', by Lord Woolton.

Originally conceived in Britain during the First World War, the National Loaf was re-introduced in 1939.

"SPAM"—is the registered trademark distinguishing the product manufactured exclusively by Geo. A. Hormel & Co. "SPAM" is made of pure pork shoulder meat with ham meat added. "SPAM" is sold ONLY in 12 OZ. tins plainly marked with the trademark "SPAM". We are sorry that during the war, supplies of "SPAM" are restricted.

★ *"SPAM" is a registered trademark*

Made from flour of 85 per cent extraction, the National Loaf was the Government's way of getting across to the public a loaf of 'the highest nutritional value'.

Unfortunately, the reappearance of the National Loaf rekindled the old 'white-versus-brown' bread controversy, which had also originated during the Great War. Those opposed to white bread had coined the slogan, 'The whiter the bread, the sooner you're dead', while the supporters of the National Loaf proclaimed that 'White bread's best; brown won't digest'.

'The result of eating white bread is pale, thin children of poor growth, and with wretchedly bad teeth', claimed the authors of the First World War publication, *National Food Fund Handbook For Housewives*. 'They are suffering, if their mothers only know it, from "white bread-starvation", the book also stated quite adamantly. 'Those families which

Bringing in the Sheaves

"Harvest Wain" 1945 model

live so largely on bread should *never* use the ordinary *white* baker's loaf. The housewife should *always* ask for *either wholemeal bread, or the old-fashioned Household Bread*. Good home-made bread is better than any that can be bought', the authors concluded with a good deal of common-sense observation.

In some areas the original National Loaf had been of doubtful nutritional merit, with certain bakers reputedly resorting to the use of alum, pipe clay and chalk in their quest for the whiter-than-white loaf. A century or so earlier unscrupulous bakers had whitened their bread with ground stone, powdered bones — and white lead.

In *Humphrey Clinker*, the 18th century writer, Tobias Smollett had observed — quite correctly, as it happened — that 'The bread I eat in London is a deleterious paste, mixed up with chalk, alum and bone-ashes insipid to the taste and destructive to the constitution'.

During the 1850's, a Dr. Arthur Hill Hassall analysed almost fifty loaves of bread from a variety of sources and not one was free from alum. Other researchers found that pub landlords 'frothed' their beer with the help of green vitriol or sulphate of iron. Cocoa powder often contained a high percentage of brick dust!

In 1860, the first British Food and Drugs Act was passed. It was revised and strengthened in 1872. In spite of regulations regarding the purity of food and the type of additives permitted, the law was often flouted in many countries. As late as 1969, an Italian was charged with selling grated umbrella handles as Parmesan cheese.

While the National Loaf of World War Two fell short of offering the benefits of the wholemeal loaf, it was still a vast improvement on earlier bread and infinitely more nutritious than the modern sliced loaf, with its countless chemical additives.

The National Loaf was finally phased out in 1953.

BRAND NAMES

Countless popular items of food became virtually unobtainable, or were only availabe on a limited regional basis, during the war — among them favourites like Robertson's Golden Shred Marmalade, Jacob's Cream Crackers, Idris Fruit Squashes, Kraft Cheese, Nescafé (only introduced to Britain from Switzerland in 1939), fresh eggs, poultry, bananas and other foreign fruit — but the housewife was left with familiar savoury aids like Bisto, Torox, Oxo, Marmite, Silvox, Verox, Beefex, Brooke Bond Beef Cubes and Bovril, with which to brighten bland meat and vegetable dishes in the absence of a knowledge of culinary herbs.

Many advertisements for meat and vegetable extracts and stock cubes at that time were a source of great amusement to children — and deliberately so. Most of these products were highly nutritious and of benefit to children particularly during wartime.

A series of advertisements sponsored by the Bovril Company in 1941 featured a delightful cartoon character in the form of a vegetable man astride a charging, snorting bull. In the foreground of the picture stood a milestone bearing the words 'To The Home Front'.

The advertisement's principal message was 'A Little Bovril Helps The Vegetables Along'. This was wartime propaganda at its most effective. One small captioned cartoon illustration contained patriotism, child-appeal and humour. It also publicized an established and highly respected brand name — Bovril — a product which had first appeared in Britain in 1886.

Bovril was the creation of a Scotsman named John Lawson Johnston, who first marketed Johnston's Fluid Beef in

Quebec, Canada, in 1874. The company set up operations in Britain a decade later and within five years had established itself as a household name under its new trade-mark of Bovril, derived from *Bos-* (Latin for ox) and *Vrilya*, the name given to the 'life-force' in a long-forgotten novel, *The Coming Race*, written by Bulwer Lytton in 1871.

Bovril has always been promoted as a 'healthy drink', as opposed to a food, and during its early history the product made use of such slogans as 'Nutritious, Delicious & Perfectly Pure' and 'The Substance of the Beef — Not The Shadow'.

In 1889, Bovril gained the Gold Medal at the International Food and Cookery Exhibition in London. Two years later, the company had become a little bolder with its advertising and a caption from that year read 'The Two Infallible Powers. The Pope and Bovril'!

During the Second World War the production of Bovril continued almost uninterrupted, in spite of the shortage of raw materials. It was highly prized for its nutritional value by soldiers and civilians, and Winston Churchill was said to have enjoyed a bedtime snack of sardines and Bovril.

The Bovril Company also published catchy little rhymes to accompany several of its wartime advertising campaigns, among them:

BOVRIL "doffs the cap" to the splendid women of Britain

The way in which women are tackling unaccustomed, strenuous and often dangerous war work, has won, and deserved, widespread admiration. As mechanics, as bus conductors, lorry drivers and porters, as W.R.N.S., A.T.S., W.A.A.F., land girls and nurses, their record of service is itself the most eloquent tribute to the women of Britain. Bovril acclaims their fine spirit.

HOT BOVRIL CHEERS!

Little cubes of carrot,
Leeks and 'taters too;
Simmered with some Bovril
Make a tasty stew.

and

Britain's boys are all born fighters.
Bovril builds the little blighters.

In 1945, Field-Marshal Montgomery paid tribute to Bovril's war services:

I am sure you will be glad to know that the assaulting troops that crossed the Rhine in the moonlight on Friday night, 23rd March, all had a drink of Bovril before starting.

Mr. Churchill much enjoyed a cup of it when touring the same area on 24th March.

Typical of Bovril's wartime messages was 'In Any Emergency Bovril Is Quick To Serve'.

The manufacturers of the enormously

successful Oxo Cube also made use of simple poetry to get their message across. The *Oxo Meat Cookery Book*, contained the following verse:

Good health is based on cookery
So scan this book with care,
You'll find good Oxo recipes
And much to help you there.

Another Oxo promotional verse was a little more imaginative and read:

A thousand years ago and more
The ox's hide was the front door
To keep out the cold.

And still today even moderns say
That Oxo is *the only way*
to keep the cold out.

Bisto was another well-established savoury aid, which made effective use of cartoon-style characters and rhymes. The remarkably successful Bisto Kids — still enjoying huge popularity in the 1980's — appealed to young and old and most certainly contributed to the war effort by boosting public morale with bright, cheerful posters and adverts. Bisto's verse of 1942 was also quite successful and captured the spirit of the times:

This is the tale of Gertrude Oat
Who never wrecked a gravy boat.

for soups and stews

Look at her gravy, can't you see?
It's just the right consistency.
It makes the most of all her joints
And meaty things requiring points.
The reason is not hard to guess,
It's Bisto gives her such success.

This particular advertising rhyme was well accepted because it openly alluded to food rationing and was directed at the very heart of the Kitchen Front.

One of the most popular vegetable products during the war, Marmite was recommended as 'essential for normal growth in children and healthy skin and teeth'.

Marketed as a savoury spread at the turn of the century, Marmite, which takes its name from the French (*petite marmite* — a clear beef broth served in a kettle-shaped pot (a *marmite*) — proved to be extremely versatile. The company issued a number of Marmite-based recipes during the war, including Potato and Leek or Onion Soup, Watercress

Soup, Curried Meat, Omelette Marmite and Potato Surprise.

Stock cubes and extracts were developed as early as the 17th century and were based on strong veal stock, which was slowly cooked for several hours, strained and simmered again. Once this initial process was completed the stock was allowed to set. It was then cleaned of all sediment and cooked again until it developed into a glue-like substance. This *veal-glue*, as it was called, was then put into little pots until quite cold and later transferred to flannel and then to paper for long storage. It apparently 'kept' for many years in this manner.

DIGGING FOR VICTORY

When manufactured food additives and savoury extracts were in short supply in the kitchen, the customary stock-pot was often brought into play and women skilled in the ways of obtaining every last ounce of goodness from meat left-overs and fresh or stale vegetables conjured up the most delicious stews and broths. Nothing was wasted. Old bones, potato peelings, pea-pods, limp cabbage and lettuce leaves and such like were all put to good and nourishing use.

Every inch of space in the garden and allotment was utilized for vegetables, salad crops, herbs and fruit.

Before the war was many months old, it became obvious that Food Rationing was not going to mean excessive hardship, because garden and allotment produce would more than compensate for any shortage of imported, commercially grown or manufactured foods.

The British Mushroom Industry advertised mushrooms as a 'War Food

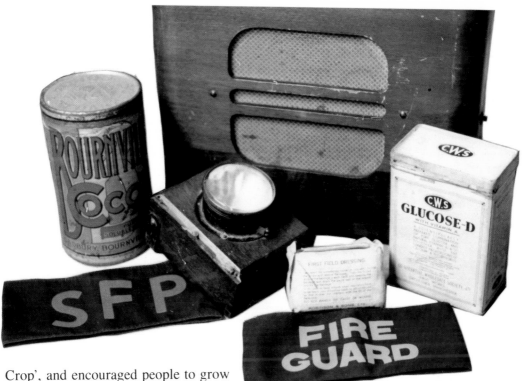

Crop', and encouraged people to grow them in their 'cellar, shed, garage, barn or greenhouse all the year round'. Mushrooms would 'happily grow in boxes in a basement room, or even behind the sofa, or under the bed if you keep them regularly watered!'

Mushrooms could, of course, be cultivated in an open garden without too much trouble.

On May 31st, 1940, the Government had ordered that 'Shelters must be up by June 11th. If you have an Anderson Shelter and have not yet erected it and covered it with earth, you MUST do so before June 11th — or give a good reason in writing to your local authority. Covering the shelter properly means covering to a depth of fifteen inches on top and thirty inches on the sides and back.'

The soil covering on an Anderson Shelter, too, could be used to grow certain produce, such as rhubarb, cucumbers and marrows.

Practical Gardening and Food Production by Richard Sudell had a chapter on 'How to Adapt Your Garden in War-Time', based on an 'ordinary' suburban plot of about 35 ft. wide, with a rear garden length of 100 ft. One half to two thirds of the garden should be devoted to the culture of vegetables, suggested Mr Sudell. A plot of this size would provide a family of four or five people with enough produce for at least part of the year. The crop included cauliflower, cabbage, Brussels sprouts, broad beans, peas, carrots, kale, broccoli, turnips, celery, leeks, beetroot, parsley and the near-obligatory potato.

There was no room for complacency in the drive to produce more food. The Government was quick to point out that the cultivation of *all* kinds of food was absolutely essential to Britain's survival.

The growing of intermediate crops, such as spinach and chives, to replace those original plants dropping out of cultivation was also encouraged to obtain the maximum efficiency from a garden or allotment.

In May 1940, the newspapers reported on the invasion of Holland under the headline of 'The Dutch Larder':

The invasion of Holland will have two important effects on the warring nations. 1. It will deprive Britain of a small but important source of food. 2. It will add to Hitler's difficulties in feeding not only his own people but those in the conquered countries.

Holland, in peace-time, was our fourth largest source of bacon. We paid her about £2,500,000 a year for it. She was our fourth largest supplier of cheese, and she came next to Denmark as a supplier of eggs. Every year we bought about 720,000,000 eggs from the Dutch and paid £2,699,000 for them. Holland was our biggest supplier of condensed milk and her exports of dairy produce to Britain were worth more than £8,500,000, a figure surpassed only by Australia, New Zealand and Denmark. Holland also sent us £2,000,000 worth of tomatoes . . .

Four weeks later, Mr Robert Boothby was quoted in the *Daily Sketch* as saying 'Not a carrot or an onion will be wasted under the Government's new emergency food scheme. Don't waste a single vegetable'.

If the invasion of Holland wasn't enough to give the Government an attack of anxiety neurosis, the German invasion of Norway added to its problems but Lord Woolton, ever the optimist, revealed no outward signs of alarm when he commented:

You need have no fear that food supplies will be seriously interfered with. Temporarily, at least, the Nazis have slammed the door of Britain's Scandinavian pantry.

In May 1942, the Government declared war on the allotment holder's arch-enemy — the house sparrow. Described by the Government as 'Hitler's Feathered Friend', the house sparrow was denounced by the Ministry of Agriculture as an 'enemy of the nation' but it warned that 'only the house sparrow is to be destroyed. The hedge sparrow is one of the most useful birds...'

Exactly how the general public was supposed to identify one sparrow from another was not made clear but one can imagine the horrendous slaughter of innocent robins, starlings, thrushes, chaffinches and other birds.

The rabbit also fell foul of the Ministry of Agriculture and in 1940 a *Daily Express* news item, 'Herr Rabbit — Fifth Columnist', reported:

The Ministry of Agriculture is calling on all farmers to wage a war on rabbits this autumn. Rabbit meat, says the Ministry, is of low nutritional value, and five rabbits will eat as much as one sheep. They damage corn and grass — in fact, they cost the nation between £30,000,000 and £60,000,000 a year. Farmers will be acting in their own interests as well as the nation's if they set to work on their own to rid their farms of these pests, agriculture's Fifth Column.

Nevertheless, rabbits were heavily featured in wartime recipe books and pamphlets and the recommended methods of cooking included frying, stewing and jugged rabbit.

With fresh eggs in short supply during the war, it was worthwhile to keep chickens if garden space permitted. Throughout the early 1940's newspapers contained advertisements claiming to have developed 'wonder egg producers' and 'egg machines'. The company producing Karswood Poultry Spice, claimed that three pullets owned by a Newbury woman had laid a total of seventy-nine eggs in one four-week period. A Crawley man using the same product reckoned to have received two hundred and five eggs in three months — from four yearlings.

Oddly enough Dried Eggs actually caught the public's imagination after a while and many people preferred them to fresh eggs.

'Eggs are a protein food, remember, and take the place of meat. And Dried Eggs have exactly the same nutritional value as shell eggs', explained a Ministry of Food advertisement.

'When the week-end joint is only a memory, when you're out of luck at the fishmonger's, or have no time for off-the-ration shopping, give your family a dish made with dried eggs. And there's no need to be apologetic about it', read another Government Dried Egg leaflet.

Keeping chickens for egg-laying was a popular wartime practice, however, and many cookery books of the period included recipes for dishes requiring fresh eggs.

The war years became a time of highly creative cooking as the direct effect of the Government's drive to make Britain a self-sufficient nation during and after the war.

The Ministry of Food was eager to learn from its own mistakes — and there were many during the first months of Food Rationing — and 'public enquiries' were held to determine the needs of housewives living in different parts of the country.

One such enquiry was held in Barrow, Lancashire, in September 1942.

Housewives and grocers were encouraged to air their grievances about the things they could not obtain — like fresh fish.

Other complaints were frequently aired in Readers' Letters columns of daily newspapers, and on BBC food programmes. In July 1943, the *News Chronicle* published a typical letter from Mrs. E.F. Bell, of Bush Hill, London, which read:

> Lord Woolton is to be congratulated on making a child's ration book available to expectant mothers. It is hoped that he will also make it possible for them (1) to obtain their oranges and fish without queueing; (2) to obtain salad and green vegetables at a reasonable price. The second point could be made if all vegetables were sold at fixed maximum prices which working-class wives could afford.

Housewives often wrote to the Ministry of Food to complain about restaurant meals not being rationed. Lord Woolton listened sympathetically before replying officially that 'The Ministry's view is that the 180,000,000 meals served in canteens and restaurants each week ensures that the worker is fed near the job'.

The nation's ingenuity in the garden, allotment and kitchen was truly amazing and reflected Britain's dogged and almost light-hearted determination not to

be beaten by Hitler.

The constant boosting of the nation's morale was an all-important factor in winning the war. The Government maintained a continous barrage of propaganda to keep the hopes of Britain's Kitchen Army held high. Housewives were made to feel that they were an integral part of the overall war effort.

If a nation ever marched into battle on its stomach, it was Britain, and the proud members of Britain's Kitchen Army are to be remembered for standing firm in the face of almost overwhelming odds with courage, tenacity and, above all, humour.

Among the countless recipes revived, adapted or created solely by the women of the Kitchen Front were those that conjured up an immediate impression of an impending victory – Blackout Cake, Commando Casserole, Tansy Pudding, Army Broth, Turnip Tommies, Dominion Pie, Guard's Pudding, Semi-Soya Pudding, Tripe Salad, French-Canadian Pea Soup, Location Loaf, National Roly-Poly, Potato Jane, Army Cake, Raid Cake, Warworker's Cake, Economy Pudding, Lord Woolton Pie and Wartime Christmas Cake.

Each one is a vivid but homely reminder of those terrible years between 1939 and 1945.

SAVE IT!

Rich and poor were brought together on a common level during the war. Food rationing and air raids affected everyone. It was as difficult at times for the middle and upper classes to manage on restricted rations as it was for the 'ordinary' housewife.

The Government did not relax its grip for one minute. It wasn't simply a case of economizing at the meal table, but of cutting back on the use of coal, gas and electricity. Posters urged people to 'Save Fuel for the Factories' and 'Cut Your Electricity and Gas – They Both Come From Coal'.

Paper, rubber and glass were recycled. Old clothes and rags were urgently needed for paper production. One reclaimed cardboard cereal carton would provide enough material for one cut-out target; six old paper bills or receipts made one washer for a shell; three shell caps could be made from a daily newspaper. The practice of giving the dog a bone to chew was discouraged; bones were needed to aid the war effort. Cast and wrought iron gates and fences were torn down and sent for scrap. Even bits of string were called in to make fire hoses.

One yard of string saved weekly by everyone in the country over the age of fourteen would have provided enough string, in a year, to stretch round the world forty two and a half times! The imported hemp required to make that much string was enough to make 200,000, hundred-foot lengths of urgently needed fire hose. Thirty three pounds of hemp made a hundred feet of

2¾ inch fire hose.

If everyone during wartime had saved just one third of a therm of gas a week in cooking, room warming or water heating, there would have been enough gas to fill nearly 14,000 large gas holders. Over 2,500,000 tons of coal were needed to produce that much gas — enough to fill a goods train 500 miles long! Not only would such a saving in domestic gas render more coal available for national use, it would have freed 5,700 trains for more essential war use.

If each family in the country collected twenty pounds of scrap iron — from old bedsteads, bicycles, worn-out garden tools, sewing machines and kitchen implements — they would have provided enough steel to build fifty new cargo ships, or more than 5,000 army tanks.

The Government also stressed that 16,000 tons of soap could be saved every year if each family used one piece less a month. Most of the fats used in soap making could be processed into edible oils. The amount of oil required to make 16,000 tons of soap could have been used to make 11,300 tons of margarine — enough to supply the fats ration to a million people.

By giving up some of the butter and fat they normally ate, people helped supply shells for the Army and Navy. A ration of 8 oz. butter, margarine and cooking fat, was only 2½ oz. below what the average person consumed before 1939, but that saving amounted to 152,000 tons of fat each year. From the amount of fat saved by the ration, 15,000 tons of glycerine could be extracted. From that much glycerine 34,000 tons of nitroglycerine could be

manufactured — and that was sufficient for use in the charges of 19 million shells! A by-product in making high-explosives from edible fats was fatty acids, used in the making of soap. One hundred pounds of fat produced ten pounds of glycerine.

By restricting fruit imports during the

DIG for victory NOW!

war the Government claimed to have saved 1,825,000 tons of shipping space annually.

Each of these savings related directly to the housewife and the Kitchen Front. It is not surprising, therefore, that the Ministry of Food and the Ministry of Agriculture waged such a relentless campaign.

But it wasn't all plain sailing and, in addition to the war itself, there were other problems to contend with. Some were the results of natural disasters, such as the failure of the West Indian sugar crop, which amounted to 70,000 tons destined for Britain. In September 1943, there was such a shortage of labour to help in the fields that the potato harvest was in in danger and Civil Servants were offered a week's special leave to help save the crop. The following year saw German prisoners digging potatoes in Eastern England to help relieve the shortage in the London area.

In January 1945, potato rationing had been unofficially introduced in many areas of Britain. The normal weekly potato consumption at that time was 6 lb a head, but this was reduced by half. Bad weather and the lack of labour and transport were blamed for the shortage.

One Brighton greengrocer said 'I have never seen such a shortage here since the last war. People are actually shop-

crawling for potatoes.'

Minor incidents, such as the loss in 1942 of 50,000 eggs destroyed in a fire at a Huddersfield packing station and directly affecting normal egg distribution in the West Riding of Yorkshire, added to the Government's problems of feeding the nation.

Harvesting Britain's food in wartime was an acute problem because of the loss of manpower to the services and industrial jobs — a total of about 50,000 men. Land Army girls, although often resented, were among those brought in as extra labour in the fields at harvest time.

To compensate, the Government increased farm labourers' wages from the nation pre-war average of £1. 7s. 10d. to £2. 8s 0d. in 1940. By 1943, the weekly wage for farm workers had risen to £3. 5s. 0d.

46

Mechanisation received a tremendous boost. 'Tractors for Britain' became a familar slogan, gaining as much prominence in the farming communities as the 'Fighting Fit' maxim elsewhere.

Old, forgotten and archaic machinery was taken out of moth balls and put to work in the fields. Rusting steam traction engines and antiquated tractors were dusted off, overhauled and used again to aid the 'big man with the plough'.

Farming methods in the British Isles had languished in the 19th century. The war dragged British agriculture into the 20th century with a vengeance.

The Sussex Downs, the Weald of Kent and the East Anglian fens went under the plough. Potatoes were grown in the hills of Montgomeryshire and transported by lorry and train to Manchester after harvesting.

Shortage of shipping had greatly affected the import of vital grain supplies to Britain and for this reason Lord Woolton was anxious that the nation should 'eat potatoes instead of bread'.

Farmers were told that there was no such phrase as 'too much'. During the war there would be no such thing as 'surplus food'; it would all be accounted for.

Lord Woolton praised the British farmers, saying:

> We tell them what we want. We pitch our requirements high. We ask what would not long ago have been thought unattainable. They do not flinch. They set about meeting our demands.

So successful was the Government's

agricultural campaign that by 1944, the Ministry of Agriculture was calling for between 500,000 and 1,000,000 volunteer workers to work on the land. 'A harvest for the people by the people', is what the Government called it.

America, taking a leaf from Britain's book, turned in enough food production in 1942 to feed an extra 20 million people. The results had been obtained without the compulsory measures existing in Britain. In Kansas, the Dakotas and Western Canada, every available space, including spare bedrooms and town dance halls, were full of wheat. But America, too, faced a serious labour shortage in the fields and had to resort to recruiting every available man, woman and child to assist with the harvest.

Total self-sufficiency was Britain's ultimate plan.

In the meantime the kitchen commandant — the housewife manning the ranks of the Kitchen Army — had to grapple with seemingly endless problems, including rationing, economy of fuel and essential commodities, and trying to make a little money go a long way. There was also the need to provide attractive, energy-making meals for the family.

Cooking during past wars had always presented the housewife with difficulties, which she overcame in various ingenious ways. But the problems arising from the outbreak of the Second World War in September 1939, were colossal by comparison. Kitchens were bombed, blitzed and burned. Gas supplies were interrupted, cooking appliances put out of action. Essential food was in short supply.

In 1941, Hilda Nield, in her excellent book, *War-Time Cookery*, wrote:

> Women who had never consciously seen their kitchen stoves have found themselves confronted by the necessity of preparing meals for their families. The ordered routine of houseproud women has been drastically cut to pieces by the coming of evacuees, refugees or billeted Servicemen and women or war workers, for whom meals have to be prepared at times which never before figured in their household curriculum.

How the Kitchen Front succeeded in the face of such adversity is one of the miracles of the Second World War.

The following collection of authentic wartime recipes spanning the years 1939-1945, is a tribute to the fighting spirit of the indomitable Kitchen Front . . .

RECIPES
FROM
THE KITCHEN FRONT

SOUPS
FISH
MEAT
VEGETABLE DISHES
PUDDINGS

ARMY BROTH

INGREDIENTS
3 small onions
3 medium carrots
1 cupful of peas
2oz washed rice
quantity of bones and meat scraps
2 tablespoons fine oatmeal
4 tablespoonfuls clarified dripping
salt and pepper to taste
2½ quarts of water

METHOD
Melt the dripping in a large saucepan. Prepare and slice the carrots and onions and fry them in the fat until browned. Add the water (or weak stock), peas, bones, scraps of meat and rice and simmer until the peas are quite soft. Remove the bones, scraping off any meat. Add oatmeal (moistened with cold water) and seasoning and cook again on a moderate heat for about 10 minutes. Serve with toasted bread.

(Serves 4-6)

BONE SOUP

Although bones were urgently needed to aid the war effort, this nourishing soup was a wartime favourite.

INGREDIENTS
3lb uncooked bones
1 carrot
1 onion
½ turnip
1 head of celery, shredded
2oz dripping
1 bay leaf
10 peppercorns
4 or 5 cloves
1 tablespoonful flour
1 tablespoonful fruit sauce or ketchup
pinch of salt

METHOD
Break or saw the bones into small pieces. Prepare and cut into pieces the carrot, onion and turnip. Melt the dripping in a saucepan and, when smoking hot, add the bones and vegetables and fry them to a good brown colour, turning occasionally. Then pour two quarts of cold water over them, bring to the boil and skim continuously. Add the bay leaf, cloves, salt and peppercorns and simmer for about six hours, skimming if required and adding more water. Strain through a sieve and allow to get cold and leave until the following day. Remove all the fat from the top of the soup, return to heat and boil. Stir in the flour mixed with sauce and celery and cook until the latter is tender. Serve hot.

(Serves 6-8)

BREAD SOUP

INGREDIENTS
3 pints of stock or pot liquor
½lb bread-crusts
salt and pepper to taste

METHOD
Break the crusts into small pieces
and place them in a basin. Boil up
the stock and pour sufficient over the
bread to cover it. Cover the basin
and allow the bread to soften, then
mash out any lumps with a fork.
Add the prepared bread to the
remainder of the stock, boil and
gently simmer for about 15 minutes,
then season to taste and serve.

(Serves 6)

CREOLE SOUP

INGREDIENTS
1 small cabbage
1 medium-sized potato
1½ gills of water
small knob of margarine
grating of nutmeg
pepper to taste
1 teacupful of milk

METHOD
Wash, trim and finely shred the
cabbage and place in a saucepan with
the water, which should be lightly
salted. Cook for about half an hour,
then add the potato, cut into thin
slices, and boil for a further 30
minutes. Mash the potato into the
cabbage with a wooden spoon until
puréed. Season well with pepper and
grated nutmeg, and add the
margarine; milk and a little more
water to bring the soup to the
required consistency. Bring to the
boil and serve hot with toasted
bread.

(Serves 4)

HERB SOUP

INGREDIENTS
1lb mixed herbs and greens —
sorrel, spinach, lettuce,
watercress,parsley, mint and thyme
1 large onion, sliced
2-3oz margarine
1oz flour or 2 egg yolks
3oz breadcrumbs
pinch of mace
salt and pepper to taste
4 pints white stock
¼ pint of cream
fresh herbs for garnish

METHOD
Wash and finely chop the herbs,
spinach, lettuce and onion. Gently
heat the margarine in a saucepan and
add the herbs and other prepared
ingredients and soften. Add the flour
and mix well together. Gradually
pour over stock, bring to the boil
and allow to simmer for about 15
minutes. Add the mace and then
sieve the soup through a fine
strainer, return to pan, add
breadcrumbs and check for
seasoning. If the addition of flour
fails to thicken the soup to the
desired consistency, mix two egg
yolks with cream and pour into the
soup. Stir well, reheat but do not
boil, and serve with a garnish of
chopped herbs.

(Serves 4-5)

ECONOMICAL CELERY SOUP

INGREDIENTS
1 small head of celery
1 onion
1oz lean bacon
¾ tablespoonful flour
½ pint of milk
½oz fat
1½ pints of water
salt and pepper to taste

METHOD
Thoroughly clean the celery and slice
it finely. Peel and slice the onion and
dice the bacon. Melt the fat in a
stewpan and fry the vetgetables in it
without browning. Put in bacon, salt,
pepper and water and simmer for
about 40 minutes, until the celery is
tender. Strain and run the soup
through a sieve and return it to the
saucepan. Add the milk and bring the
soup to boil. Mix the flour with a
little milk, gradually stir into the
soup and let the mixture boil gently
for 5 or 6 minutes. Season to taste
and serve.

(Serves 3-4)

STORK MARGARINE
COOKERY SERVICE

PEA-POD SOUP

Absolutely nothing was wasted during the war and pea pods, which are double-skinned, could be separated, the inner skin discarded and the remaining outer skin could be used in salads, or cooked to form the basis of a soup. During the 1800's street vendors sold 'hot pease-cod' — peas boiled in their pods, dipped in hot butter and seasoned with salt, vinegar pepper and drawn through the teeth (or squeezed with the fingers) to extract the peas. The same vendors also sold pease porridge from heavy tin containers. The porridge eventually became known as pease pudding and was served with hot boiled salted beef or pickled pork. The familiar rhyme, 'Pease Pudding Hot', dates from around 1797.

INGREDIENTS
1lb pea pods
2 onions
2 or 3 sprigs of mint
small bunch of parsley
1 handful of spinach leaves
1 teaspoonful sugar
1oz flour
½ pint of milk
a few fresh peas for garnishing
2 pints of bone or vegetable stock
salt and pepper to taste

METHOD
Wash the pods well and put them in a pan, together with the stock and chopped onions, and simmer for approximately one hour, until tender. Add the mint, parsley and spinach to cook during the last ten minutes. Sieve or press the mixture through a sieve or colander, leaving only the papery part of the pods and stalks of mint and parsley behind. Mix the flour and milk smoothly in a pan, add the sieved soup, sugar, seasoning and fresh peas. Simmer until the peas are tender, stirring frequently, and serve hot.

(Serves 4-6)

PINK POTATO SOUP

Probably of mid-Victorian origin, this attractive-looking soup was especially popular with children during the war — for obvious reasons.

INGREDIENTS
1lb raw potatoes to each cup of soup
1 small leek or onion
1 small cooked beetroot
a little fat for frying
salt and pepper to taste

METHOD
Heat a little fat in a saucepan and add finely grated raw potato and leek or onion. Fry and stir for a few moments, then fill the saucepan with boiling water, or vegetable liquor. Season with salt and pepper and continue to cook until the potatoes have cooked almost to a mash. Chop the beetroot as finely as possible and add to the soup. Re-heat and serve piping hot with toasted bread or rolls.

(Serves 4)

RABBIT SOUP

INGREDIENTS
1 rabbit
1 small onion
1 carrot
½ head of celery
1 dessertspoonful mushroom ketchup
2oz fat
1 quart of stock
salt and pepper and herbs to taste

METHOD
Prepare and wash the rabbit well before cutting into joints, keeping the liver apart. Fry the joints in a little melted fat. Put the fried joints, liver and stock into a saucepan and simmer for about one-and-a-half hours, skimming well. Take out the back joint of the rabbit, cut off some of the meat and put the bones back into the soup. Add the onion, carrot and celery (chopped finely) and herbs to taste. Season with salt and pepper and simmer for one hour. Strain the soup, rubbing the liver through a sieve, return to the saucepan and add the mushroom ketchup. The meat taken from the back should now be cut into small pieces and added to the stew. Gently re-heat and serve hot with toast.

(Serves 4-6)

POLISH BARLEY SOUP

INGREDIENTS
1 quart of vegetable boilings (liquor)
1oz pearl barley
1lb mixed vegetables — potatoes, carrots, swede, turnips, celery, parsnips, spring onion or leek, kale, cauliflower and mushrooms (the stalks will suffice)
chopped parsley
a little milk
pinch of salt

METHOD
Prepare and dice/chop the vegetables in the boiling salted liquor with the barley until tender. In Poland sour cream would be added but milk will be sufficient. Pour in the milk, stir the soup and maintain steady heat. Serve with toast, oven-dried rusks, or crisp rolls. This soup is intended as a main-course!

(Serves 6-8)

STRAIGHT-FROM-THE-GARDEN SOUP

This recipe was created by the Ministry of Food during the early years of the war.

INGREDIENTS
4oz shelled green peas
3oz French beans
2 young turnips (about 2½oz)
1 onion
2oz lettuce
3 tender carrots (about 2½oz)
3oz spinach
1½oz rice
sprig of mint
1 quart of vegetable liquor
salt and pepper to taste

METHOD
Wash and prepare the vegetables, dicing the root vegetables and slicing the beans. Bring the stock to simmering point and add the vegetables, mint and rice and boil for approximately 20 minutes, or until tender. Season well, remove the mint and serve hot.

(Serve 4-6)

POTTED BLOATERS

INGREDIENTS
4 large bloaters
1 teaspoonful anchovy essence, or sauce
1½oz margarine
freshly ground black pepper to taste
cayenne pepper to taste

METHOD
Put the fish onto a baking tray and cook in a hot oven for 20 minutes on Regulo 6. Cool the fish slightly and then carefully remove the skin and all bones while it is still warm. Beat the bloaters until quite smooth and add the anchovy essence/sauce, peppers and softened margarine and beat in thoroughly. Put the resulting paste into china or glass containers and use a little melted butter to seal the contents. Store in a cool place until required.

(Serves 4-6)

STUFFED BAKED COD
with PARSNIP BALLS

Publicised as a 'New Fish Dish', fresh-salted cod was also widely promoted as being 'grand for children as well as grown-ups and what a bargain!' At 9d a pound cod did represent good value for money in war-time.

INGREDIENTS
2lbs middle cut of cod
1½ozs breadcrumbs
1 teaspoonful chopped parsley
1 teaspoonful mixed herbs (such as rosemary and thyme)
1 tablespoonful chopped suet
egg or milk to bind
salt and pepper to taste
a pinch of onion powder (made from dried onion skins)
dripping for basting

METHOD
Wash the fish and remove the bones. Mix the dry ingredients for the stuffing and bind with the beaten egg or milk. Fill the fish with the stuffing, and tie up securely with thread. Brush over with egg or milk, coat lightly with browned breadcrumbs, and place in a baking tin with sufficient dripping for basting. Cook in a moderate oven for 30-40 minutes, basting well. A rasher of fat bacon may be placed on the fish when cooking. Serve with anchovy or brown sauce and parsnip balls.

PARSNIP BALLS

INGREDIENTS
1lb parsnips
quantity of breadcrumbs
salt and pepper to taste

METHOD
Wash and peel the parsnips and boil in a little water only. Mash well and season with salt and pepper. Shape into balls, roll in the breadcrumbs and bake in a hot oven for 20 minutes, either with the fish or in a dish by themselves.

(Serves 4)

BAKED COD'S HEAD

INGREDIENTS
1 large cod's head
4oz breadcrumbs
3oz chopped suet
1 teaspoonful chopped parsley
a little grated lemon rind
salt and pepper to taste
milk to moisten
a little margarine
a little chopped onion

METHOD
Thoroughly wash the cod's head and place it in a deep fire-proof dish. Make some veal stuffing with breadcrumbs, suet, parsley, lemon rind and seasoning and enough milk to moisten. Put the stuffing into the hollow of the cod's gills, season the fish with salt and pepper and a little chopped onion. Add some bits of margarine and a gill of water and bake in a hot oven for 10 minutes, basting the head well. Remove from oven, cover the cod's head with breadcrumbs and return to the oven until thoroughly cooked.

(Serves 1-2)

COD'S ROE ON TOAST

Recommended by the Ministry of Food as an ideal breakfast snack.

INGREDIENTS
1 small tin of cod's roe (or fresh roe)
2 small onions
2oz margarine
2 tablespoonfuls breadcrumbs
4 rounds of toast spread with butter or margarine
cayenne pepper

METHOD
Chop the onions finely and fry them in the margarine. As soon as they are browned, stir in the breadcrumbs. Drain the liquid from the roe and remove any skin. Add the roe to the onions and breadcrumbs and heat thoroughly, stirring all the time. Spread the mixture on the rounds of toast and sprinkle with cayenne pepper before serving.

(Serves 2)

HERRINGS IN BATTER

INGREDIENTS
1 tin of herrings in brine
4oz flour
1oz dripping
1oz dried whole egg powder
1 teaspoonful baking powder
½ pint water
pinch of salt

METHOD
Reconstitute the dried egg with the water in the normal way and then add the sieved flour and salt. Mix well together until the mixture is smooth. Beat well and then leave to stand for at least 25 minutes. Put the dripping into a baking tin and heat in the oven. In the meantime add the baking powder to the batter mixture and beat well. Place the herrings into the dripping and pour the batter mixture over them. Bake in a hot oven (Reg.6) for about 25 minutes and serve immediately.

(Serves 2)

HERRING PIE

INGREDIENTS
½lb grated raw potato
½lb grated raw apple
1 chopped onion
¼ teaspoonful nutmeg
4 boned herrings
1 teaspoonful lemon juice (or rhubarb juice)
6oz pastry
salt and pepper to taste

METHOD
Grease a shallow dish and arrange half the potato, apple and onion on it. Sprinkle on the nutmeg, seasoning and lemon/rhubarb juice and lay the herrings on top. Cover with the remainder of the potato, apple and onion mixture. Roll out the pastry, cover dish with it and bake in a hot oven for 30 minutes. If desired, garnish with finely chopped parsley.

(Serves 2-3)

AUSTRALIAN PIE

INGREDIENTS
1lb cold roast mutton
1oz dripping
4 Oxo cubes
1 large onion
enough slices of bread to cover when crumbled
2 tablespoonfuls of flour
1 egg (reconstituted)
½ pint of milk
½ teaspoonful baking powder
salt and pepper to taste

METHOD
Put a few slices of mutton at the bottom of a good sized pie-dish and sprinkle with minced onion, pepper and salt, and cover with bread. Repeat the process until the dish is full. Spread the top layer thickly with dripping and then moisten the mixture with half an Oxo cube mixed with hot water. Mix the remaining Oxo cubes with half-a-pint of hot water and make into a batter with flour, milk and baking powder; pour into the pie-dish and bake in a moderate oven for three-quarters-of-an-hour.

(Serves 3-4)

BACON & EGG PIE

This recipe was first published by the Ministry of Food in 1943 and was a great wartime favourite.

INGREDIENTS
2 eggs (reconstituted)
2 rashers of bacon
8oz potato pastry
½oz breadcrumbs
salt and pepper to taste

METHOD
Beat the egg. Line a plate with half the portion of potato pastry (see: Potato Flour). Mix the egg, breadcrumbs, salt, pepper and bacon (chopped into small pieces) together, then pour the mixture on to the plate and cover with remainder of potato pastry. Bake in a moderate oven for half-an-hour and serve hot or cold.

(Serves 2)

BACON & SEMOLINA

INGREDIENTS
2ozs semolina
1 gill household milk
3 gills water
1oz margarine
3ozs bacon
salt and pepper to taste

METHOD
Prepare the semolina overnight as follows: Put the milk and water into a pan and bring to the boil. Sprinkle in the semolina stirring as you do so. Add the margarine and seasoning and cook for fifteen minutes, stirring frequently. Turn the mixture into a shallow dish and leave until morning. Cut the semolina mixture into medium slices. Fry the bacon lightly, remove from heat but keep hot. Fry the semolina slices in the bacon fat until golden brown, turning them over when one side is done. Serve on a hot dish with the bacon on top.

(Serves 1)

59

BUBBLE & SQUEAK

A traditional 19th century dish, the name of which derives from the sounds emitted when cooking. During the 1800's, an unknown poet penned these lines in praise of the dish:

When midst the frying pan, in accents savage,
The beef so surly, quarrels with the cabbage.

An early Victorian method of making the dish was as follows:

INGREDIENTS
A few thin slices of cold beef
butter
cabbage, 1 sliced onion
pepper and salt to taste

METHOD
Fry the slices of beef gently in a little butter, taking care not to dry them up. Lay them on a flat dish, and cover with fried greens. The greens may be prepared from cabbage sprouts or green savoys. They should be boiled till tender, well drained, minced, and placed till quite hot in a frying pan, with butter, a sliced onion, and seasoning of pepper and salt. When the onion is done, it is ready to serve.

The wartime variation was less sophisticated and a typical recipe from the period reads:

INGREDIENTS
2 to 3ozs beef dripping
several thin slices of roast beef, cold boiled beef, or pork
any kind of cooked green vegetables, such as spinach, cabbage or mashed peas
mashed potato
½ onion, finely shredded
salt and pepper and herbs to taste

METHOD
Dissolve the dripping in a frying pan and add some of the slices of cold meat and fry until golden brown. Mix together the other ingredients in a separate dish and then add them to the pan, stirring continuously until brown on both sides. Serve piping hot with a dash of Worcestershire sauce to enhance the flavour.

(Serves 2)

COMMANDO CASSEROLE

INGREDIENTS
1lb potatoes
1lb parsnips
1 leek or small onion
1lb sausage meat
1 teaspoonful vegetable or meat extract dissolved in a teacupful of water
½ teaspoon-thyme
pinch of sage
salt and pepper to taste

METHOD
Shred the cabbage very finely and slice the remaining vegetables as thinly as possible. Roll the sausage meat out on a floured board and cut into four pieces. Grease a casserole dish and put in alternative layers of vegetables and sausage meat and season with salt, pepper and other herbs. Let the first and last layer of the dish be potato slices. Pour in the gravy, place lid on the casserole and cook in a moderate oven for thirty minutes. Remove the lid and dot the potatoes with dripping and return to the oven — with the lid off — for a further twenty minutes.

(Serve 6-8)

DOMINION PIE

INGREDIENTS
¾ lb potato pastry (see: Potato Flour)
1lb sausage meat
1lb of any raw green vegetable, such as cabbage, or spinach
2lb of cooked haricot beans
a few bones for stock
1 meat cube, or 1 teaspoon of yeast extract

METHOD
Line an 8-in. cake tin with most of the potato pastry, keeping back enough for the lid. Divide the sausage meat into two halves and form into two flat cakes, placing one at the bottom of the tin and adding shredded green vegetables and cooked beans. Season. Place the second sausage meat cake on top of the first. Damp the top edges of the pastry with water and place the pastry lid firmly in position. Cut a small hole in the top to allow the steam to escape, and bake in the oven (Reg. 7) for 20 minutes, and Regulo 5, for a further 25 minutes. When cold pour a little concentrated meat stock made from the bones and flavoured with the meat cube, or yeast extract, through the hole. Allow to set and serve cold with salad and salad dressing.

(Serves 6-8)

LIVER OMELETTE

INGREDIENTS
¼ lamb's liver
2 rashers of bacon
2 eggs
½ pint of milk
salt and pepper to taste
1oz butter

METHOD
Chop the liver and bacon into tiny pieces. Beat the eggs well (using reconstituted dried egg if necessary), mix with the milk and season with salt and pepper. Butter, rather thickly, a pie dish, turn the omelette into it and bake in a hot oven for about half-an-hour.

(Serves 1-2)

LOBSCOUSE

So called because of its Liverpool-Irish origins ('scouse') and the slang term for meat, 'lob', the dish is said to have been the creation of 17th century settlers in Lancashire. Lobscouse became a popular dish with the British Navy in 1942.

INGREDIENTS
1lb mashed potatoes
2 or 3 tinned or bottled
tomatoes, cut into pieces
3oz grated cheese
2 tablespoonfuls of milk
1 nut of margarine
salt and pepper to taste

METHOD
Melt the margarine in a small saucepan, then add the grated cheese and milk. Stir over a low heat until the cheese is melted, then add the mashed potatoes and tomatoes and continue to cook gently until the ingredients are blended, stirring continuously. Season with salt and pepper and serve on a bed of piping hot mashed potatoes.

(Serves 2-3)

PLOUGHMAN'S PIE

A tangy, fulfilling dish that must have been greatly appreciated at the end of a long day in the fields, particularly at a time when labour was in short supply owing to the demands of war and industry.

INGREDIENTS
½lb cold beef
½ teaspoonful curry powder
½ teaspoonful grated nutmeg
1 finely chopped onion
½ carrot, chopped or grated
2 tablespoonfuls chopped
parsley
½ pint of vegetable or rice
stock
½oz margarine
salt and pepper to taste

METHOD
Remove all fat, skin and gristle from the meat and chop it roughly. Put the meat into a basin and mix it thoroughly with the carrot, parsley, nutmeg and curry powder. Fry the onion in a little margarine until brown and soft and stir in with the

other ingredients. Season carefully and pour in enough stock to make the mixture quite moist — like thick porridge.

Short Pastry

INGREDIENTS
½lb self-raising flour
3oz margarine
pinch of salt
water to mix

METHOD
Sift the self-raising flour and salt together, rub in the margarine and mix with cold water to make a stiff, dry paste. Knead lightly until smooth and roll out to an oblong shape. Put the meat mixture into a pie dish and damp the edges of the dish. Cover with pastry, make a hole for the steam to escape, trim and decorate the edge with the prongs of a fork, and bake for 30 minutes in a moderately hot oven (Reg.6). Serve hot.

(Serves 2-3)

SAILOR'S PIE

This was intended as a dish for a large family, or the mess on board a small ship.

INGREDIENTS
1½lbs. stewing steak
2lbs small onions (one stuck with three cloves)
1lb tomatoes
6 carrots
1 bay leaf
2 tablespoonfuls vinegar
2oz margarine
salt and pepper to taste
1 quart of water

Seasoned Flour

INGREDIENTS
2 tablespoonfuls flour
1 teaspoonful salt
½ teaspoonful pepper

METHOD
Mix together thoroughly.

Crust

INGREDIENTS
¾lb self-raising flour
4oz margarine
pinch of salt
cold water to mix

METHOD
Sift the flour and salt together, rub in the margarine and mix to a stiff dough with cold water. Knead together until smooth on a floured board and roll into a round to fit just inside a casserole.

METHOD
Cut the steak into small squares, removing all fat, and roll in seasoned flour. Skin any fat from the steak and melt it in the casserole, adding the margarine. Cook the steak in the hot fat until brown on all sides. Add onions, tomatoes (quartered), scraped carrots cut into small pieces, vinegar and bay leaf, and season with salt and pepper. Bring slowly to the boil and simmer on a low heat, or in a moderate oven for 3-4 hours (Reg.3). One hour before the dish is ready to serve, put the crust over the top and cook in the steam from the stew.

(Serves 10)

FADGE (Irish Potato Bread)

INGREDIENTS
2lbs. potatoes
salt
measure of flour

METHOD
Scrub and boil the potatoes in their skins. Drain and dry over a low heat and mash with a fork while still hot. Allow to cool until the little finger can bear the heat of the potato. Add a pinch of salt and work in enough flour to make a pliable dough. Knead well on a heavily floured board. Roll out to about ¼-inch thick and cut into wedge-shaped pieces. Cook on a hot-plate, or hot girdle, or in the oven until brown. Turn and brown on the other side.

(Serves 4-6)

TRIPE & ONIONS

INGREDIENTS
1lb tripe (enough for 4)
3 tablespoonfuls finely minced onion
a little flour
1oz dripping
½ pint stock
1 gill of milk
salt and pepper to taste

METHOD
Wash and prepare the tripe and then cook in the usual way. When tender, cut the tripe into convenient pieces. Melt the dripping in a saucepan and, when hot, add the onion and cook slowly until gently browned. Add the flour and mix in well with a wooden spoon. Stir in the stock, milk and seasoning and bring to the boil. Put the pieces of tripe into the sauce and simmer for about 15 minutes.

(Serves 4)

LORD WOOLTON PIE

Possibly the most famous of all World War Two economy dishes and reputedly created by Lord Woolton himself, the Pie was actually conceived by the Chef of London's Savoy Hotel and made no use of parsnips in the original recipe. The original Lord Woolton Pie, as published in *The Times*, was as follows:

Take 1lb each diced of potatoes, cauliflower, swedes and carrots, three or four spring onions, if possible one teaspoonful vegetable extract and one tablespoon of oatmeal. Cook all together for 10 minutes, with just enough water to cover. Stir occasionally to prevent the mixture from sticking. Allow to cool; put into a pie dish, sprinkle with chopped parsley, and cover with a crust of potatoes or wholemeal pastry. Bake in a moderate oven until the pastry is nicely brown and serve hot with a brown gravy.

If the wartime housewife was short of fat, the following pie-crust pastry could be made without fat:

INGREDIENTS
8oz wheatmeal flour
1 level teaspoonful baking powder
a pinch of salt
a pinch of powdered sage, if desired
¼ pint of cold milk, or milk and water

METHOD
Mix the dry ingredients together, then stir in the cold milk and water. Knead the mixture until a dough-like consistency is attained. Roll out the pastry and use it as you would an ordinary crust.

The contents of Lord Woolton Pie could be varied according to the seasons. As alternatives, cooks could use turnips, parsnips, cabbage and mushrooms with the potatoes.

Another potato dish inspired by Lord Woolton and using the potato for both filling and crust, was called, appropriately, 'Inspiration Pie'.

(Serves 8-10)

FRIED LEEKS

INGREDIENTS
1½lbs medium-sized leeks
4 tablespoonfuls olive oil or lard
1 clove of garlic
1 bay leaf
4 large tomatoes
salt and pepper to taste
1 teaspoonful lemon or rhubarb juice

METHOD
Prepare the leeks in the usual way and cut into one-inch lengths. Heat the oil or lard in a large frying pan and add the leeks. Skin and crush the garlic and put it into the pan, together with the bay leaf, and cover the pan and simmer for 20 minutes. Drop the tomatoes into boiling water, then remove the skins. Chop the tomatoes finely, add them to the leeks and season with salt and pepper and cook for a further ten minutes, stirring occasionally. Stir in the lemon/rhubarb juice and serve hot.

(Serves 4)

OSLO SANDWICH

INGREDIENTS

8 thin slices of bread (to make 4 sandwiches)
2 skinned tomatoes
several lettuce or cabbage leaves
2 large radishes
2oz grated cheese
salt and pepper to taste
margarine for spreading on bread
salad dressing

METHOD
Leave the crusts on the bread and, if possible, use thinly-sliced cabbage leaves rather than lettuce, as cabbage eaten raw is much richer in Vitamin C. If you have it to hand, also include some coarsely-chopped parsley, as this is also rich in Vitamin C. Spread the bread with margarine, then put in three layers of filling (between the four slices), using cheese for one filling, tomatoes for another, and cabbage or lettuce moistened with salad cream and sprinkled with salt for the third. Cut the two four-decker sandwiches diagonally across (making four sandwiches in all) and secure each with little pins made from cocktail sticks, or even a clean used matchstick, with half a radish as a head.

(Serves 2-4)

POTATO CUTLETS

INGREDIENTS

1lb potatoes
1 breakfast cup of breadcrumbs
4oz liver sausage, or cooked
sausages
1 peeled onion
1 dessertspoonful chopped
parsley
1 beaten egg (reconstituted)
a little fat
salt and pepper to taste

METHOD

Thoroughly clean, peel and boil the potatoes in the usual way. Mash thoroughly with a fork and add the breadcrumbs, retaining a quantity for later. Remove skin from sausages (unless using cooked sausages), chop into small pieces and add them to the other ingredients. Chop the onion and parsley finely and add them to the mixture. Season to taste and bind the mixture with the beaten egg. Leave the mixture until quite cold and then shape into cutlets, brush with beaten egg, roll in breadcrumbs and fry in hot fat, or bake in a hot oven until browned. Serve and eat piping hot.

(Serves 2-3)

POTATO FLOUR

The true versatility of the potato manifests itself in the making of this flour. Potato flour was particularly recommended during wartime and while its preparation is a fairly lengthy and tedious process, the results are more than satisfying.

INGREDIENTS

3lb peeled potatoes
1½ pints cold water

METHOD

Pour ½ pint of water into a mixing bowl and grate the potatoes into it. In order to achieve a really fine potato mince, use the small holes in the grater, or put them into mincing machine and pass them through twice. Do this so that the potatoes are grated directly into the bowl, so that no juice is lost.

Place a piece of fine muslin over another basin and pour the grated potato and water mixture into it and rinse them (still in the muslin) in another bowl containing a fresh ½ pint of water. Again press out all the liquid from the cloth and add to this the first batch of liquid. Repeat this process with a further ½ pint of water and add this to the pint you already have. The basic idea is to thoroughly rinse the gratings of 3lb of potatoes using altogether 1½ pints of water. *No potato gratings should be allowed to get into the liquid.* The mixture should now be left to stand for several hours — and it will turn black!

Now pour the liquid from the starch, which has now fallen to the bottom. This is the foundation of *potato flour*. It looks dark grey in colour because it is still wet. Spread the flour on to a small plate or saucer and leave to dry overnight. Rub or shake through a sieve and only store when completely dry.

To use for thickening, stir one dessertspoonful of *potato flour* with two dessertspoonfuls of cold water and add to ½ pint of hot liquid, according to how firm you require the finished dish to be. For custard use colourings and flavourings in order to give your dish a familiar look.

SCOTCH NETTLE PUDDING

INGREDIENTS
2 heads of broccoli
¼ lb rice
2 good-sized leeks or onions
1 gallon of young nettle tops
pinch of salt

METHOD
Thoroughly wash the nettle tops, discarding any ragged leaves. Clean and finely chop the broccoli and leeks/onions and mix with the nettle tops. Place them altogether in a muslin bag in alternate layers with the rice and tie the bag tightly. Boil in salted water long enough to cook the vegetables; the time varying according to the initial tenderness of the vegetables. When cooked serve with gravy or melted butter.

(Serves 4-5)

SAXA SALT

FREES DRY & FREE-RUNNING

The best packet salt in the World

BRITISH MANUFACTURE

Put more Flavour and Richness into your Meat Dishes by using Saxa Your Grocer Sells it

1½d and 2½d

TATTIE HUSHIE

An early Caledonian leek and potato dish featured in a number of wartime cookery books.

INGREDIENTS
1 ½ lbs diced potatoes
1 large sliced leek
2oz butter or margarine
1oz medium oatmeal
2 pints milk
salt and pepper

METHOD
Clean the leek well to remove all traces of soil and soot, and simmer with the diced potato in boiling water to cover, until tender. Drain and mash thoroughly with butter or margarine. Stir in the oatmeal, milk and seasoning, then place on heat until just below boiling point, stirring continuously. Serve hot with a dash of ketchup, or brown sauce, if preferred.

(Serve 3-4)

TOMATO PANCAKES

INGREDIENTS
4oz plain flour
1 level teaspoon of salt
1 egg
¼ pint of milk, or milk and water
1oz grated cheese
8ozs skinned and chopped tomatoes
2 teaspoonfuls chopped parsley
lard for frying
tomato sauce for serving

METHOD
Sift the flour and salt into a mixing bowl and make a hollow in the flour and add the egg. Mix in the egg and gradually beat in the milk, or milk and water. Stir in the cheese. Mash the tomatoes and blend with the parsley and add them to the mixture. Heat a little lard in a frying pan until it begins to smoke and add enough of the batter to cover the base of the pan. Fry until golden brown underneath and then turn the pancake and cook similarly the other side. Keep the pancake hot on a plate over a saucepan of simmering water while you cook the remaining batter. Serve hot with tomato sauce.

(Serves 2)

VEGETABLE PUDDING

INGREDIENTS
1lb potatoes, peeled and finely grated
1lb parboiled mixed vegetables, such as carrots, parsnips, turnips, celery, onions and swede
a quantity of vegetable liquor
½lb flour
2oz fat
1 teaspoonful vegetable or meat extract
salt and pepper to taste

METHOD
Mix the grated potato with flour and add salt, pepper and vegetable/meat extract. Rub the fat into this and add enough cold vegetable liquor (the water used to parboil the vegetables is ideal) to make a firm dough. Thickly grease a pudding basin and line it with the potato dough, reserving some for the cover. Fill the basin with the parboiled vegetables and use the remaining liquor to make a gravy and pour into the mixture. Cover with the reserved potato dough and steam or boil in the normal way for 50 minutes to an hour.

(Serves 3-4)

VICTORY SALAD

INGREDIENTS
*1 pint of diced, boiled potatoes
1 cup of diced, boiled beetroot
½ tablespoonful minced onion
(wrongly printed in one
contemporary cookery book as
'mined' onion)
¼ cup of French dressing
1 cup of shredded cabbage
1 cup of cooked, sliced runner
beans
a little chopped parsley or
paprika
salt and pepper to taste*

METHOD
Stir all the ingredients together in a
large bowl, using a wooden spoon,
and add the beetroot last. Moisten
the salad with dressing and serve
with cold meat, or as a course in
hors d'oeuvres.

(Serves 4)

WHEATMEAL CARROTS

INGREDIENTS
*½ lb carrots
1 tablespoonful grated stale
cheese
1 tablespoonful chopped parsley
1 large cupful of browned
wheatmeal breadcrumbs
a little chopped onion
salt and pepper to taste
1 tablespoonful wheatmeal flour*

METHOD
Scrub the carrots, slice lengthwise
and cook in salted water until tender.
Strain and put aside. Mix the cheese,
parsley, breadcrumbs and chopped
onion with half a large
breakfastcupful of carrot water.
Season to taste and heat through.
Blend 1 tablespoonful of flour with
the remainder of the carrot water,
stir into the cheese mixture and
simmer for five minutes, stirring
constantly. Pour the mixture into a
shallow casserole, cover with a thick
layer of cooked carrots, cover with a
lid and bake in a moderate oven for
a quarter of an hour.

(Serves 1)

BELGIAN EGGS

Ingredients

2 eggs (reconstituted)
2 medium potatoes
1 small onion
1½oz margarine
1 teaspoonful chopped parsley
salt and pepper to taste

Method

Mince the onion and fry in margarine in a small saucepan. Cut the potatoes into half-inch cubes and brown in the pan with the onions. Lift out the potatoes and onions and drain off the fat. Beat the eggs and cook in margarine, stirring until they are just beginning to set, then add the potatoes, onion, parsley and seasoning. Serve with or on toast spread with dripping. If desired add grated cheese.

(Serves 2)

CHEESE GIBANICA

Ingredients

2oz flour
½lb mashed potatoes
knob of fat
1 teaspoonful dried egg
sugar to taste
small amount of grated cheese
pinch of salt
a little milk

Method

Make a dough from the flour and water, adding a pinch of salt. Put the prepared dough into a floured cloth and leave to set for an hour. When the dough is ready, roll out thinly and pull out until it is as thin as paper and leave to dry in a warm room. Make a mixture of the mashed potato, dried egg, sugar, a little milk and fat. Cut the pastry to fit snugly in a tin. Put in alternate layers of pastry and filling, sprinkling each layer of filling with a little grated cheese. Make the top layer of pastry and bake in a moderate oven for 30 minutes.

(Serves 1-2)

BARA BRITH (Welsh Bread)

INGREDIENTS
8ozs self-raising flour
juice and rind of 1 lemon
1 rounded teaspoonful mixed spice
4ozs currants, or sultanas
½ level teaspoonful bicarbonate of soda
3oz margarine or cooking fat
¼ pint of milk
2 tablespoonfuls sour milk
1 heaped tablespoonful black treacle or syrup
pinch of salt
1 level tablespoonful dried egg (optional)
4oz brown sugar
1 heaped teaspoonful of caraway seeds

METHOD
Sieve together the flour, dried egg, spice and salt and then rub in the margarine/fat. Stir in the sugar, fruit, caraway seed, lemon rind and juice. Slightly warm the treacle or syrup, mix with the milk, stir in the bicarbonate of soda and quickly stir into the flour. Put the mixture into a well-greased 2lb bread tin and bake for one-and-a-quarter hours on the middle shelf of a moderate oven (Reg.4).

BREAD PUDDING

INGREDIENTS
1lb stale bread
8oz mixed dried fruit
3oz chopped suet
¼ level teaspoonful salt
2oz chopped mixed peel
1 level teaspoon ground cinnamon
½ level teaspoonful ground nutmeg
3oz soft brown sugar
1 large egg (or reconstituted)
a little milk

METHOD
Reduce the bread to small pieces and cover with cold water and steep for 30-40 minutes. Squeeze the bread as dry as possible and place in a large bowl. Beat in the remaining ingredients and mix well. Put the mixture into a large greased baking tin and smooth the top. Bake in a moderate oven (Reg.5) for 2-2½ hours until the top is crisp and golden. When cold sprinkle with castor sugar, cut into squares and serve. If desired serve hot with custard.

(Serves 3-4)

GUARD'S PUDDING

INGREDIENTS
1 beaten egg (reconstituted)
3oz stale breadcrumbs
3oz finely chopped suet
2 tablespoonfuls jam
1 teaspoonful browning
1 tablespoonful flour

METHOD
Mix together the breadcrumbs, suet
and flour and moisten with the egg,
jam (warmed slightly) and browning.
Turn into a greased basin, cover with
greased paper and steam until set.

(Serves 1)

APPLE BLOSSOM
FRITTERS

This simple and delightful recipe can be
traced back to the reign of Edward III
and was a great favourite in the royal
household.

INGREDIENTS
Several apple blossoms
a rich batter
fat for frying

METHOD
Simply wash the apple blossoms,
shake them dry, and coat with batter
and fry for a few minutes.

(Serves 2)

PARKIN

INGREDIENTS
½lb fine oatmeal
½lb flour
4oz brown sugar
4oz treacle
¼oz ground ginger
1 teaspoonful pepper
2 teaspoonfuls baking powder
2oz butter
a little milk

METHOD
Mix together in a basin the oatmeal,
flour, ground ginger, pepper and
baking powder. Put the treacle, sugar
and butter into a saucepan and warm
until well mixed. Stir in the dry
ingredients making a smooth dough,
and adding a little milk if required.
Pour the mixture into a greased
Yorkshire pudding tin, which has
been lined with grease-proof paper,
and bake in a steady oven.

(Serves 4)

POOR MAN'S ICE CREAM

INGREDIENTS
1oz arrowroot
4oz condensed milk
*2 breakfastspoonfuls boiling
water*

METHOD
Mix the arrowroot to a smooth paste
with a little boiling water, then add
to it rather less than two
breakfastspoonfuls of boiling water
and stir until it thickens. Cool and
then add the condensed milk. Stir
thoroughly, flavour to choice and
freeze.

(Serves 1)

DRIED EGG CUSTARD

INGREDIENTS
2 level tablespoonfuls dried egg
1 level tablespoonful sugar
2 level tablespoonfuls flour
5 level tablespoonfuls powdered milk
1 pint of water
a little grated nutmeg

METHOD
Mix the dry ingredients together, then blend with a little cold water to make a thin cream. Boil the rest of the water and pour slowly onto the egg mixture, stirring well all the time. Put the mixture into a saucepan, bring to the boil and cook for 2-3 minutes. Add the nutmeg and serve with steamed pudding or stewed fruit.

(Serves 2-3)

JUNKET

This was a summer favourite and although it was possible to purchase bottled junket mixes, many housewives preferred to make it the traditional way, which is as follows:

INGREDIENTS
1 pint of milk
1 tablespoonful castor sugar
1 teaspoonful plain rennet
1 or 2 bay leaves
a little grated nutmeg

METHOD
Warm the milk to blood temperature, stir in the sugar, rennet and bay leaves and pour into a basin. Sprinkle with nutmeg and leave in a warm room for half-an-hour, or until set, but remove bay leaves before setting occurs. Serve with jam or cream. *Note*: The milk *must not boil*, or the junket will not set. Ensure that the bay leaves are removed carefully, otherwise the junket may curdle.

(Serves 2)

SEMI-SOYA PUDDING

One brand of soya flour, 'Soyolk – The Pioneer Edible Soya Flour', was marketed with a leaflet containing numerous recipes, which included: Scotch Shortbread, Bakewell Tart, Marzipan, Malt Squares, Soya Crispie, Basic Steamed Pudding and Welsh Rarebit.

Soya flour, it was stressed, 'should be used in conjunction with National flour, cornflour, or other cereal flour for the best results.' Soya contained twice the protein of meat, and four times that of wheat. This particular recipe was therefore extremely nutritious and popular during the war.

INGREDIENTS
2 dessertspoonfuls semolina
2 dessertspoonfuls soya flour
1 dried egg (reconstituted)
1½oz sugar
2 teaspoonfuls custard flavouring, or other preferred flavouring
1 pint of milk

METHOD
Mix the semolina, soya flour and sugar together and blend into a smooth paste with egg and a little milk. Bring the remainder of the milk to a boil, pour over the mixture and add flavouring. Return the mixture to the saucepan and stir over a gentle heat until it thickens. Pour into a greased dish and bake for 30 minutes in a moderate oven.

(Serves 2)

TANSY PUDDING

INGREDIENTS

3oz white breadcrumbs
1oz sugar
½oz butter
2 eggs (reconstituted)
½ pint of milk
1 dessertspoonful finely chopped tansy leaves

METHOD
Boil the milk and pour over breadcrumbs and leave for one hour. Beat the eggs and add the sugar and tansy leaves and mix with the breadcrumbs. Add the butter and blend in thoroughly. Bake in a pie dish in a moderate oven until set. Serve cold with a little sugar and cream.

(Serves 2)

STEWED DANDELIONS

INGREDIENTS
1 bunch of young dandelions
2oz butter or margarine
1 tablespoonful flour
stock as required
salt and pepper to taste

METHOD

Wash the dandelion leaves thoroughly and drain and boil in a little salted water. Cook until tender, stirring occasionally. Remove from heat and hold them under cold running water to prevent them from becoming unpalatable. Put a piece of butter/margarine into a saucepan and slowly melt. Add the flour and stock (the water in which the dandelions were cooked will suffice), stir well until smooth and then add the dandelion leaves, salt and pepper. Cook for a further 10 minutes, stirring frequently.

(Serves 2)

WARTIME CHRISTMAS PUDDING

A few minor sacrifices had to be made with the egg, milk and sugar ration for this recipe but the end result made it totally worthwhile.

INGREDIENTS
½ lb flour
4oz sugar
½ lb chopped, stoned dates
¾ lb shredded suet
grated nutmeg
1 pint of milk or beer
2 tablespoonfuls lemonade
½ lb breadcrumbs
1lb stoned raisins
½ lb sultanas
½ teaspoonful salt
3 eggs (fresh or reconstituted)
1 teaspoonful baking powder

METHOD
Mix all the dry ingredients together first. Beat the eggs and add to the mixture. Add the lemonade, milk/beer and stir until the ingredients are well blended. Put into a well greased basin, cover with greaseproof paper, then with scalded, floured pudding cloths, and boil for 8 hours.

(Serves 8-10)

WARTIME FRUIT LOAF

INGREDIENTS
6oz margarine
8oz sugar
½ lb ground rice
½ lb flour
6oz sultanas
6oz currants
a little chopped lemon peel
1 teaspoonful bicarbonate of soda
½ pint of milk

METHOD
Put the flour and ground rice into a mixing bowl and rub in the fat and other dry ingredients. Stir the baking soda into milk and then mix it in with the other ingredients. Put the mixture into a greased tin and bake in a moderate oven for 2 hours.

WAR & PEACE CHRISTMAS PUDDING

No, not a Tolstoy special, but a seasonal pudding devised by the Canadians during the First World War and revived in Britain at the end of 1939. Take note that the ubiquitous potato has crept into this interesting recipe, together with Dr. Carrot.

INGREDIENTS
1 cupful flour
1 cupful breadcrumbs
½ cup suet
½ cup mixed dried fruit
1 teaspoonful sweet mixed spice
1 cupful grated raw carrot
1 cupful grated raw potato
1 level teaspoonful bircarbonate of soda
2 tablespoonfuls hot water

METHOD
Mix together the flour, breadcrumbs, suet, mixed fruit and spice. Then add the grated potato and carrot, bicarbonate of soda and thoroughly mix in the water. When the mixture has attained the correct consistency turn it into a well greased pudding bowl — but ensure that it does not reach more than two-thirds full. Boil or steam for a least two hours.

(Serves 6-8)

WARTIME TRIFLE

INGREDIENTS
4 small tea buns
fruit juice, either bottled, cooked, or very thin apple juice;
thin custard made with custard powder or potato flour and flavouring (see: Potato Flour).

METHOD
Cut the buns across and put them into a large dish and soak with fruit juice. Pour a little thin custard over it and top with a little fruit if available. *OR*: Soak the buns with thin custard, pour the fruit juice over, and use fruit for the final decoration.

(Serves 4)

BEETROOT JAM

INGREDIENTS

1½lbs raw beetroot
6ozs (about 3 large
tablespoonfuls) syrup
3 rounded tablespoonfuls sugar
3 tablespoonfuls fruit squash or
cordial
red colouring
plenty of fruit flavouring such
as pineapple, or raspberry

METHOD

Wash the unpeeled beetroot
thoroughly, peel thinly and trim off
the parts not required. Rinse once
more and then cut into long pieces
about one inch thick. Put these
through a mincer by inserting the
points of longish pieces first. Make
sure that all pieces of beetroot,
minced and otherwise, are kept on
enamelled or china plates to avoid
staining. You can also *grate* the
beetroot if preferred.

Put syrup and sugar into a fairly
large saucepan and boil until slightly
brown. Add the minced beetroot with
all the juice — it ought to be about
one-and-a-half inches deep. Stir until
the mixture starts to boil again, cover
with a lid and adjust the heat so that
the jam will continue to boil gently.
After twenty minutes boiling, add the
squash, colouring and flavouring.

Now taste the jam! If the little bits
are fairly soft, continue to boil
without the lid. If they still seem
hard, cook for a while longer with
the lid on. In any case, you should
cook the jam for 10-15 minutes
without the lid on. Check for
flavouring again. Remember to stir
the jam from time to time and
always smooth the top of the mixture
when you continue boiling to ensure
an even substance when cooked. This
jam is *not* a preserve but it will keep
in a cool place for almost two
weeks.

WORKINGMAN'S PUDDING

Originated in Yorkshire and noted for its economy.

INGREDIENTS
1 cup of plain flour
¼ cup of brown sugar
1 cup mixed dried fruit
1 level teaspoonful ground mixed spice
1 cup boiling water
1 level teaspoonful bicarbonate of soda
1 dessertspoonful margarine

METHOD
Mix the ingredients together and beat well. Put the mixture into a well greased basin and cover with floured, pleated muslin (to allow for expansion) and boil for two hours. Serve with jam or hot custard.

(Serves 2)

WARTIME VINAIGRETTE

INGREDIENTS
2 dessertspoonfuls salad oil
4 dessertspoonfuls vinegar
pinch of dry mustard
a good shake of pepper
pinch of salt

METHOD
Mix together smoothly the mustard, pepper, salt and salad oil, then add the vinegar by gradually dropping it from a teaspoon, stirring continuously and the mixture is perfectly blended.